An Undesirable Element
An Afghan Memoir

AF499494

First Draft Publishing/*Originals*

Sharif Fayez: An Undesirable Element
An Afghan Memoir
Ryan Crocker: Foreword

Published in Germany in 2014 by First Draft Publishing GmbH, © Sharif Fayez 2013

Foreword: © Ryan Crocker 2013
Editors: © Matthew Trevithick 2013

ISBN 978-3-944214-18-4 *(softcover)*
ISBN 978-3-944214-17-7 *(kindle)*
ISBN 978-3-944214-19-1 *(epub)*

Cover Photography: © Philip Poupin
www.philippoupin.fr
Concept & Design: Bureau Christoph Dunst
www.christophdunst.com
Cover Design: Bureau Christoph Dunst
Typefaces: Heimat Mono *www.atlasfonts.com* & Arnhem
www.ourtype.be

All rights reserved. Alle Rechte vorbehalten.
First Draft Publishing GmbH, Berlin – printed in Germany.

www.firstdraft-publishing.com
info@firstdraft-publishing.com

Table of Contents

Foreword 7

Early Life 13

College Life 16

First Return 21

Poetry and a PhD 23

Herat Destroyed, Life Destroyed 26

Crossing Into Iran 32

An Undesirable Element 35

Afghan Collapse 48
The Soviet withdrawal 49
Mujahideen 50

Taliban 54

The Change 57
My involvement in Bonn 61

The Minister of Higher Education 63
The State of Higher Education in Afghanistan 64
Private Universities 71
Women's Education 72

Pakistan 76

Epilogue 78
The American University of Afghanistan 78
The Taliban and the Future 81
To the Diaspora 81

Ryan Crocker: Foreword

I can distinctly remember the way Kabul looked in January 2002, when I helped reopen the US Embassy after it had been closed for more than a decade. At the time, I compared it to Germany after World War II, and with the city's infrastructure completely destroyed, it was an apt comparison.

While I worked to determine how best to help rehabilitate Afghanistan, just down the road, another man was working from impossibly modest facilities (even, briefly, a hotel room) to develop an education strategy for the country. Sharif Fayez, a reluctant Afghan academic-turned-government servant working as the minister of higher education, had simple and restorative ideas: education should be supported and nurtured, and made a cornerstone of the new Afghanistan. At a time when most of us were addressing an astonishing list of short terms issues, he took the long view and realized that education – higher education in particular – would be absolutely critical to recreating an Afghanistan based on freedom, respect, peace, and inquiry.

As he makes clear in the following pages, that Afghanistan is the Afghanistan of his childhood. He begins right at the start, walking us through a simple and peaceful upbringing centered on poetry and academic performance, and provides warm descriptions of his experiences as he becomes a college student at Kabul University in the capital.

Receiving scholarships to study for his master's and doctoral degrees in the United States, he writes at length about his observations of life in America, some of which reveal our foibles (including his surprise at Columbia University's unkempt dormitories, which leads him to think he's not attending a very good school and to transfer to a school in Colorado). Ever the poet, his doctorate proves the direct influence of a 13th century Persian poet on the famed Walt Whitman, linking the US and Afghanistan to the surprise of his colleagues.

The warmth of these stories contrast, sadly, with his painful descriptions of Afghanistan as it slides towards violence and extremism, which he saw from his perch as a professor at Kabul University. Hunted by the government, he flees to neighboring Iran only to find himself in the midst of the Iranian Revolution and the subsequent Iran-Iraq War, where he makes a living teaching English and literature at a university in impossibly trying circumstances before eventually being deported.

Eventually returning to the US, he emerges as a powerful voice of reason against the infighting plaguing Afghanistan after the Soviet withdrawal and, ultimately, against the Taliban government. After the liberation of Afghanistan in 2001, he learns that he is a minister in the new government by watching the BBC and seeing his name scroll across the screen. Reluctantly, he accepts the position and works to restore Afghanistan to the country he knew as a child, navigating a sea of obstacles to reopen universities across the country shuttered by fighting and extremism and enroll the first students – male and female - committed to creating a new Afghanistan. After his term finishes in 2004, he stays on to help create the American University of Afghanistan, now entering its eighth year of operation with more than 1,000 students from around the nation.

Although Professor Fayez's goal may have been to restore the world of Afghan education he knew in his youth, he actually went far beyond that. He is the primary architect of a progressive, liberal education system, both public and private, that Afghanistan has never known. I have had a number of AUAF and Kabul University graduates; they will transform their country. And they are the best single guarantee that the Afghanistan of the future will never again resemble its dark past.

While largely a story about the remarkable life of Sharif Fayez, ultimately, this is also a tale about the power of vision and dedication – and the ability to make a difference. I hope you enjoy it as much as I have.

Ryan Crocker

US Ambassador to Afghanistan 2011 - 2012
Dean, Bush School of Government and Public Service
Texas A&M University

An Undesirable Element

Early Life

My name is Sharif Fayez. In 1946, I was born in a small village in Herat, a province of Afghanistan that borders Iran. The village is called Seeyoshan, and it's a beautiful area with fruit trees located between a river and a desert. Peoples' lives are intricately connected to the earth, and their days spent planting, growing and harvesting grapes and fruit.

The river, one of the biggest in the country, is called the Hari Rood, and it flows through the Herat Valley from east to west. People living close to the river work in rice paddies when the river is full, while people on higher ground maintain their orchards. During my childhood, cars could not make it into the village because there were no bridges strong enough for them over our hundreds of creeks and streams, though they can now. Later, when the Soviets occupied the area, they found the terrain so difficult that, when sweeping for mujahideen, they simply asked the people to come out of their homes by loudspeaker and bombed the village from the air if they refused.

In the evenings, after a long day in the fields, people would come back from their fields and go to sleep early. We were farmers, and it was a simple life. There were no refrigerators, so we stockpiled our dried fruit and dried meat in bags for the winter. On most weekends, we would take our produce to sell in the market in the city, and buy sugar, cooking oil and tea there.

There was one good elementary school in the area, located five kilometers away amid orchards and green fields. There were no buses, and only one person near the village owned a car. Our entertainment on weekends was often going to watch for the car driving in one direction, and then amusing ourselves for hours until we saw it return.

We got to school by crossing dozens of little streams. This was difficult during the spring season because they were always flooding. If the creeks overran their banks, we tried to jump over them, but one of us always seemed to lose a shoe or their lunch in the water, or fall in. The streams coursed through private farmland for many kilometers, but nobody ever paid us any mind as we walked through their property. Our families were good friends. We all knew each other.

One memorable day, the last king of Afghanistan came to visit our school. King Zahir Shah was a wise and peaceful man. There were no soldiers or guards, as he had no need for protection from his people. He was wearing a suit. The school principal asked me to write a paragraph in Pashtu to be read in front of the King. I didn't speak much Pashtu at the time, but the rulers of Afghanistan have always been ethnic Pashtuns, from Ahmad Shah Durrani, known as the Father of the Nation, straight through to today. So I prepared a paragraph, and read it to him in front of the school. He was so impressed, and I remember being impressed with him because he treated all of the children like members of his family. He kissed them on their heads, listened carefully to them, praised the school principal, and encouraged us to work hard and receive top marks.

I listened to him. I emerged from that school as the top student. I received a scholarship to attend a very good school in Kabul, Avicenna High School, located then and today across the street from Kabul University. Avicenna is the Latin transliteration of the name of the brilliant philosopher and polymath, Ibn Sina, who lived in Bukhara in the 900s, in what is today Uzbekistan. His contributions to medicine, philosophy, science, astronomy, logic, mathematics and poetry made him the most famous thinker of the Islamic Golden Age one thousand years ago. His father was from Balkh, one of the oldest cities in Afghanistan.

Avicenna High School, in the nation's capital on the other side of the country, was all new for me. There were paved roads and a few cars, which we would look out for because it meant the King was nearby. We would walk to restaurants where they played Indian music and drink tea. We didn't have much money so that was our only choice for entertainment.

I mixed with students from every corner of the country. They arrived from villages in the Wakhan Corridor, which touches China, and villages in Helmand, on the border with Pakistan. Being kids, we mixed without regard to our ethnicity. We constantly made fun of each other for our different accents, customs and traditions, but we were never serious. We had differences, but it was enjoyable having classmates from around the country. We were all friends, and worked hard. Some of my classmates are top people in the government today.

Religion was relaxed. Many students prayed frequently, but the idea of a religious police that would force everyone into the mosque, which was only a few decades away from coming to my country, was laughable. We listened to the mullahs when we were in the mosque. We also listened to the radio, which picked up only one station, Kabul Radio.

Getting to the school from Herat was difficult, particularly during the winter. Though today it takes less than an hour to travel there by plane from Kabul, it took us several days. There was no paved road. If the rivers were flooding and the bridges were swept away, we had to wait until the waters receded. We brought heavy blankets to sleep on out under the stars.

The first American I ever saw was President Eisenhower, who visited Afghanistan while I was in school. The principal announced to us that instead of morning classes, we would be lining the road and waving flags to welcome an American president to our country. I was so excited. I had heard about America in my classes but never seen an American. His car drove by and I saw him smiling and waving to us. He looked friendly.

I graduated top of my class from Avicenna and was admitted to the Teachers' Training College, one of the best schools in Kabul. From there I transferred to Kabul University's School of Education, where I would meet many more Americans as my professors.

My life at Kabul University's School of Education continued much the way it had at Avicenna High School. Life was simple and peaceful, and Kabul University, opened in 1946 to succeed Kabul Medical School, which started in 1932, was quickly becoming a university that was attracting students from around the region. King Zahir Shah worked hard to forge partnerships with universities in Europe and the US. We had quite a number of them. Teachers College Columbia University, in New York City, was one. They taught English, both grammar and literature, and worked to improve the university's academic quality. The US government donated a state-of-the-art dormitory in the 1960s that I enjoyed staying in. It is still there today. Most interesting for us was seeing our first African, who was the head of the English department, on loan from Indiana University. More fascinating for us was that he was blind and taught via braille, but still had a PhD. Everybody loved him and his patience, and he fascinated us with tales from around the world. There were other partnerships as well. While Columbia University helped run the English department, Washington University developed and ran law programs, and Purdue University provided advice on how to develop the agricultural program. German universities helped teach science and economics, and several French universities sent professors as well. In my building alone, Americans taught on the first floor, Egyptian Sharia scholars taught on the second floor, and German economists taught on the third floor. It was quickly becoming a metropolitan campus. With the international faculty came new projects, new buildings, and new ideas.

I grew close to an American professor, an old woman from

California who commanded immense respect on campus. Her name was Dr. Escher, and she had a master's degree from Oxford University and a PhD from Stanford University. I worked as her assistant in her office, and she constantly encouraged me to do my very best. She was the first in a long line of Americans who would go out of their way to help me. She told me that if I did not get a scholarship to study in the US, she would pay for my education abroad out of her own pocket.

Like students in Afghanistan today, we all wanted to go study in the US. We had no computers with which to learn about America, only the stories of our professors, who were excellent ambassadors for their country. We knew little more than it was a superpower and that you could get a good education there. Coming back to Kabul with a degree from an American university was a mark of status. With that you could get a good job teaching English, which would bring a good salary.

I passed the admissions tests to attend the American University of Beirut, the closest American university, but Dr. Escher told me to wait for the results of my application to Columbia University. I trusted her, and waited for one year. During that time I worked in her office. I eventually received a scholarship, with Dr. Escher's help, from USAID to pursue a master's degree at Columbia University in New York. While I was so happy to be going to the US, I was not excited that my scholarship said I had to study linguistics. I had always hated linguistics as it didn't comprehend emotion or passion, and focused only on the rigid study of language. My passion was literature, which Dr. Escher had helped cultivate. Reading great masterpieces of literature had always sustained me.

I left the country for the first time in 1970. I was twenty four years old. Getting to the US was not easy at that time. I traveled first to Iran, where I took a Pan-American flight from Tehran to London in the United Kingdom. I stayed for one night in London at a simple hotel. In my room there was a box in the corner, which I knew from the stories of my Western professors had to be a television. It was the first time I had seen one. I fiddled with it until it turned on, and barely slept that night, transfixed by this machine. London, with its airplanes, trains, TVs and well developed roads, was something indescribable to a simple villager from a simple country.

I did not learn that Columbia University was one of the best schools in the world until after I had transferred from it. The school and I did not get along well. Part of it was New York City, which overwhelmed me. There were so many people, moving so fast, and nobody really seemed to know anybody else. It was also the dorm, which was dirty and full of cockroaches. Even though my family lived in mud huts in a rural village in a poor country, it was always much cleaner than anything I saw in New York. The combination of my living situation and the city in general made me start thinking about transferring. Suffering through a semester with a British professor from Oxford teaching Shakespeare, which my advisor had allowed me to take even though it had nothing to do with linguistics, made me determined to leave. He was a famous professor, but completely inaccessible. Students were allowed only one office visit per semester. I started thinking a smaller school would be better, lost as I was among 150 fellow students in his class. Lastly, I simply could not understand his British English.

There were a few other Afghans at Columbia at the time. All of us would go on to shape our country in one way or another, but one would shape it for the worse. Hafizullah Amin, who was seeking a PhD, would eventually lead a Communist revolution, become the president of Afghanistan by ordering the murder of his colleague, and successfully convince the Soviet leadership to invade Afghanistan in support of his regime. He would later be assassinated by Soviet commandos. Another Afghan PhD candidate, Ghafoor Ghaznawi, was one of the finest scholars I have ever met. He would eventually become the Deputy Minister of Education after the fall of the Taliban. He warned us to stay away from Hafizullah. We all knew he was a Communist. Ghafoor told us that Hafiz had established links with Cuban Communists and had a life-size picture of Fidel Castro in his apartment. He also said Hafizullah would never receive his PhD, a predication that would prove true. We kept our distance.

In my second semester, I went in desperation to my advisor. I told him I needed to transfer, that I was not enjoying my time in New York City. He told me it was clear that I needed to be in a place that was similar to Afghanistan, and suggested I go to school in Colorado. He recommended I transfer to the University of Northern Colorado, where James Michener, author of that classic book on Afghanistan, Caravans, had studied. I said I would love to transfer to Colorado, knowing little about it. I thought that if Columbia didn't have enough money to clean the hallways, how good a school could it be? It must be ranked near the bottom, because a top school would be clean.

I landed in Denver, Colorado, that same year and immediately felt better. I had arrived there by bus, and taken what would become one of the best trips of my life: a three day trek from New York City to Denver across the Midwest. The endless expanse was so beautiful, so rich, and so clean. I was enchanted. The weather was almost the same as Kabul, and the mountains provided a sense of comfort and filled me with thoughts of home. My first meeting at the University of Northern Colorado was with the chair of the English department, a man named Dr. Cross. His first question after meeting me concerned my departure from Columbia. Why had I left? Didn't I know it was a great school? I said I was surprised to hear that.

I told him I wanted to study literature, now freed from the conditions of my USAID scholarship because I was not at Columbia. He said I was not allowed to, explaining that they had admitted many foreign students to study literature, particularly from Asia, and all of them had failed. Eventually the English department passed a rule saying that no foreign students could study literature. I asked him to give me a trial period, and if I scored highly, to let me study it. He consulted with his colleagues, and they let me take three literature courses on the condition that I receive a B or better in all three. One would be the hardest course I would ever take, a study of John Milton's Paradise Lost, which examined closely ten thousand lines of verse written in fifteenth-century English. The other course was a study of Shakespeare's tragedies, and the last was a course in English romantic literature. I did not sleep much that semester, but received As in all three courses. He smiled when he told me I would be permitted to attempt my master's degree in literature. I received it in 1972.

I really enjoyed living in Colorado. It was beautiful, with clean air and mountains everywhere, just like Afghanistan. The University of Northern Colorado had a beautiful campus. The food was great, and the people were very nice.

I felt so safe. While a student, I rented a small apartment in the bottom of a house, and when I went to ask the landlord for the key, he replied, what key? I asked if I needed a key to my apartment, or if there was another locking mechanism. He told me that people here don't use keys, that his whole house was unlocked. He told me the entire city was unlocked. I was amazed.

Having finished my master's I made plans to return to Kabul, to teach at Kabul University. I had no idea how much things had changed in Afghanistan in just the two years I was away.

First Return

While I had been studying literature in the US, Communism had begun to take root in Afghanistan. When I returned in 1972 and began teaching literature at Kabul University, I noticed alarming changes.

The country, despite being years away from a full Soviet invasion, had changed dramatically. Kabul University had become noticeably radicalized. For the first time in the university's history, violence was a major problem on campus, with clashes regularly erupting between two groups that had formed seemingly overnight. One group was the Communists, and the other group the religious fundamentalists. Everything became political, and everything became ideological. These were not ethnic clashes. There were members of every ethnicity on both sides.

Both sides used arguments from literature printed in foreign countries, the Communists from books printed in the Soviet Union and the fundamentalists using books printed in Egypt and Pakistan. While both types of books were freely available, the ubiquitous nature of Soviet literature, purchaseable for less than a piece of bread and incessantly promoting revolution, led me to conclude that a systemic campaign of attempting to convert Afghans into loyal Communists was underway.

The increase in clashes led to a sharp decrease in foreign professors, who for the first time began leaving the country. The pragmatic political middle ground, historically the home of all Afghans, was shrinking as students quickly chose sides. The Communists appeared to have the upper hand, with Kabul University turning steadily into a recruiting center for young Communists, who passed out propaganda and held rallies. With the foreign professors leaving, highly educated Afghans too began considering fleeing their country, fearing, as I was, that a Soviet invasion was imminent. We were convinced that the Soviets in Moscow wanted to turn Afghanistan into another Soviet satellite like Tajikistan.

While teaching literature, I again came face to face with Hafizullah, still dedicated to turning Afghanistan into a Communist state. Kicked out of Columbia University's PhD program and having failed to write his dissertation, he was applying to teach at Kabul University. I sat on his review board, the recruitment committee. He made an eloquent pitch to be considered for a faculty position, but I voted strongly against him, leading a movement of other professors. We ultimately denied him a teaching position. Though personally disagreeing with his well known ideological views, I based my decision on an old Kabul University rule. It said that if you are given a scholarship to go study abroad and fail to receive that degree, you cannot teach. He was very angry with me. That was the last time I saw him.

I began thinking of returning to the US to pursue a PhD degree. I had three jobs during those years in Kabul. I was working at the US Information Service, working with USAID, and working at Kabul University. By working all three jobs, I earned about $1,000 dollars a month. That was a very good salary in those days.

I got married in 1973 and had my first child in 1974, which helped raise my mood despite what I saw happening to my country. I told my wife to begin to take English class, so that she could accompany me if I were accepted to study for a PhD in the US. I doubted I would be accepted as I had very little money to pursue my own studies, now raising and supporting a family.

In 1974, I learned about a scholarship that would cover all of my costs, something called the Centennial Scholarship that was being awarded by the Asia Foundation. I thought my odds of receiving it were low because they were giving out only three scholarships across all of Asia. Nonetheless, I applied, and to my great surprise was one of the three recipients. I was elated. I planned my return to the US.

Poetry and a PhD

I was admitted to study at the University of California at Berkeley, and would have loved to study there, but I was told the Asia Foundation didn't have the money to send me. They proposed the University of Arizona, in Tucson. I accepted, and began studying literature for my PhD and oriental studies for my minor. This was a time when people were very much interested in Buddhism, mysticism, and the Orient, so I decided to study it as well.

My wife joined me, but eventually longed to return to Herat. I begged her not to go, telling her that everybody was talking about a Soviet invasion and how the country was becoming more and more Communist. She asked me then, as she still asks me now: How do you know? I told her everyone knows. Afghanistan is a weak country, with a weak government, and already the university and the armed forces are full of Communists. They have already infiltrated, I told her. Sooner or later there will be war, and you will be stuck there and I will be stuck here. She left regardless.

I began pouring all of my energy into my PhD. I had become inspired by an exchange with a professor of poetry, who forcefully argued that Walt Whitman was a homosexual. It was a weird interpretation to me, because if Walt Whitman was a homosexual, then, using his definitions, most of Persia's greatest poets would be homosexuals simply because they discussed male beauty. Rumi is suddenly a homosexual and Saadi of Shiraz is as well. I told him I was constantly reminded of Rumi when I read Walt Whitman, and informed him that the grace of Persian poetry is that the great poets never allowed themselves to be constrained by the traditional definitions of anything, including beauty. Beauty would not be restricted only to women. Beauty could be something very inclusive, very cosmic.

He was a very nice person, and our conversation ended with him recommending that I write my dissertation about our conversation. I said I would, and later presented an outline to him, which he accepted.

My hope was to prove that the best American poet had been influenced by a Persian speaking poet from Afghanistan. Specifically, I wanted to find proof that Walt Whitman had read Rumi, because there were many scholars who at that time were saying that while there were some similarities, Whitman could not have read Rumi because no translation of Rumi's work in English was available during Whitman's life. If that failed, I would address the subject of how two poets from such different eras and backgrounds could produce such similar work, of the same temper.

To the surprise of everyone, I found that key piece of evidence, forever linking the best American poetry to a timeless Persian poet born in Afghanistan. The link was a book of poetry in German, by a great scholar named Rückert, who had translated some of Rumi's poetry. This book had in turn been translated into English by a man named William Alger, in a volume called Poetry of the East. I found it on the back of Walt Whitman's library checkout card, discovered after months of searching. The first entry in the book is a poem from Rumi, though because his name was kept in German, as Galalageen Balki, it was hard to understand it was really him. I knew it was Rumi after reading the first verse.

Walt Whitman had checked this book out dozens of times, reading it through again and again. He also read it out loud to soldiers wounded in the US Civil War. His service was reading poetry to dying soldiers, and he carried the book from the library to the hospital to the battlefield and back.

The first two parts of my dissertation were published by the Walt Whitman Review. Another piece was published by Comparative Literature.

Even though my research had been repeatedly verified by experts, I was still nervous as I prepared for my dissertation defense meeting. When I walked in the door, there was applause and a big party congratulating me. They said because my research had all already been published in professional journals, there was no need to check anything. It was a truly great moment, and I was awarded my doctorate.

My happiness at receiving my terminal degree would quickly fade. Less than three months after being awarded my doctorate, Soviet-supplied warplanes would savagely bomb my beloved Herat city at the orders of my Communist classmate Hafizullah Amin. Reading stories reporting more than 20,000 dead, coupled with the cessation of letters from my wife, I feared for the worst.

Herat Destroyed, Life Destroyed

On April 28, 1978, the Afghanistan that I knew and loved was swept away forever in a revolution whose consequences continue to touch every Afghan even today. Mohammad Daud Khan, the Afghan prime minister who had ended the monarchy in Afghanistan by bloodlessly overthrowing his first cousin and brother-in-law Mohammad Zahir Shah in 1973 and become president, was assassinated by army units loyal to the Communist Hafizullah Amin. My old classmate from Columbia had succeeded. Daud Khan had seen trouble coming from the Communists, but had reacted slowly, and ultimately only placed Hafizullah under house arrest. Hafizullah ordered Daud's assassination and the violent overthrow of the government from his house. Daud, along with at least six members of his family, were executed and thrown into a mass grave.

While Hafizullah was the chief architect of the coup d'etat, a man named Nur Mohammad Taraki became the leader of it, with the help of a third staunch communist named Babrak Karmal. Taraki immediately introduced sweeping and vast reforms of the Afghan state, designed from the bottom up to transform Afghanistan quickly. Among all of the policies initiated, Taraki's attempts to reform the ownership of land across Afghanistan, which in practice amounted to simply seizing land without compensation and redistributing it, set off a firestorm of resistance. There were two results: crippling food shortages in a country where the vast majority of the economy had always centered around farming, and the stirrings of resistance against the government.

Now officially Communist, the Afghan government spent much

of its first year in power crushing rebellions. One of the largest was in my city, Herat, though there were others in Jalalabad, Mazar e Sharif, and even Kabul. The Herat rebellion involved the mutiny of government soldiers as well as a popular uprising against the Communist government.

The Afghan government's response to all uprisings, in keeping with the advice they received from their Soviet advisors, now in Afghanistan in large numbers, was overwhelming force. And so, on orders from Hafizullah Amin, loyal army units were sent from Kandahar to Herat, their tanks driving on a new cement road built by Soviet engineers. Tricking the rebelling soldiers by arriving near the city with Qurans in hand and waving green flags, indicating they were joining the resistance, they drove straight into the city. There, they first massacred the mutinous soldiers from behind, and then set about crushing the uprising. Using Soviet-supplied airplanes from a nearby airbase, they bombed the city indiscriminately until the resistance stopped. By the time the bombing and shooting stopped, more than 15,000 civilians were dead.

While Moscow and Kabul contemplated what this uprising meant for international Communism and the future of Afghanistan, I knew only that the letters from my wife had stopped coming. I was completely distraught, and immediately made plans to leave the US and travel back to Afghanistan.

My professors and colleagues in Arizona pleaded with me not to go. They said I was making an irrational choice. I replied that until I knew where my wife and children were, I would not sleep. This did not deter them, and they struggled in vain to keep me in the US, out of harm's way. I traveled first to Washington, DC, to gather more information on what was happening. The head of my department at the University of Arizona, a man named Cecil Robinson, arranged for Dennis DeConcini, one of Arizona's senators, to meet with me and tell me not to go. Cecil followed this by securing me a job at Voice of America, designed to keep me in the US. I refused.

Through the State Department, I managed to send questions to the US Embassy in Kabul, which replied that it was safe for me to return to Afghanistan. They argued that since my former colleagues and classmates were in the government, it would not be dangerous for me. I didn't tell them that these colleagues had become radicalized by Communism, and were more dangerous than ever. I began my travels back to Kabul, giving Cecil only a vague promise that I would contact him if I needed to escape Afghanistan.

I barely recognized my country when I landed in Kabul in 1979. There were Soviets, mainly Russian, everywhere. I immediately got into trouble with them. The Soviets working in the airport customs office were suspicious of my typewriter. They repeatedly asked me what it was. I repeatedly told them it was a typewriter. They asked if I were sure it was a typewriter. At this point I chuckled, which got me into even more trouble. They began to take it apart. I reiterated that it was simply a typewriter. The Russian on the other side of the desk stopped taking it apart and stared at me for several long minutes, saying nothing. I held his gaze. He eventually decreed that I would be free to pick it up in a week, but for now they were going to keep it. I said ok.

The Afghan man sitting next to him, representing an Afghan ministry, collected my passport, following a procedure that did not allow Afghans to leave the country unless officially authorized. I would never see it again.

I went to check into a hotel in downtown Kabul. The first question the desk attendant asked me was if I was from Herat. I said I was. He looked around the hotel quickly, with a panicked expression on his face. He said he was going to get his manager. His manager came, and repeated the question. I again said I was from Herat. The manager shook his head and asked if he could talk with me privately. I had no idea what was happening.

In his office, the manager asked if I knew what had happened in Herat recently. I said I had heard stories. He told me, quietly, that people were talking about more than 20,000 dead, with the entire city in flames. He then told me that after the incident in Herat, the police, army and intelligence services were constantly coming through all the hotels in Kabul, asking if anyone from Herat was staying in them. He encouraged me to leave as quickly as possible, and to stay with friends. I left the hotel, and checked the situation at a hotel down the street. The manager there told me the same thing. I traveled to a friend's house and spent the night there. My friend was so angry I had returned to Afghanistan.

The next day I reported to Kabul University. I had to start working there in order to get a local passport, like in the Soviet Union, which I needed to travel to Herat. I went to an old friend's office, the head of the English department. We began to discuss current affairs over tea, and the conversation went nicely until I used the word coup, discussing the coup in 1978. His face went white, and he stopped talking. He whispered quietly, don't say the word coup. I asked what word I was supposed to used to describe what had happened in 1978. He said only use the phrase popular revolution. I said it was a textbook coup. For your own safety, he said, you should not use the word coup. We sat in silence. I looked out of his office window and saw a line of Soviet advisors walk by, and began to understand just how much things had changed.

The next conversation I had at Kabul University nearly resulted in my death. On my third day back at Kabul University an old colleague asked if I wanted to have tea with him. I could tell he was ambivalent about the situation of the country. It was common knowledge that he was the nephew of Babrak Karmal, one of the leaders of the new government, and then he did not like Hafizullah Amin or Nur Mohammad Taraki.

In his office he went off on a short rant about the incompetence of Amin and Taraki, and about the Soviets crawling over his campus. I said nothing, having nothing to contribute to the conversation. After about 30 minutes, I excused myself and left the room.

When I went back to campus the next day, the head of the English department found me and was extremely concerned. He told me that after the conversation with my colleague the day before, state intelligence had come to campus and dragged him into a car. The room had been wired. Everybody else assumed I had been taken as well. I told my boss that I didn't say anything in the conversation. He urged me stay away from the Communists. If someone related by blood to the new regime was not safe to speak his mind in a closed space, there was no hope for anyone else.

Three days later, the professor who had been dragged away was executed.

This changed everything for me. What had until now been a passionate but unfocused anger towards the Communists became personal. I could put a face to the the list of victims. I could talk about his life and tell you how much sugar he had put in his tea on his last day.

The next day I was having another conversation with a trustworthy colleague about our families when a friendly but unknown colleague walked into the room. My friend, clearly joking, asked this man if he could search him. The man smiled and said no. My friend reached out his hands to imitate patting him down. He discovered a listening device, switched on.

There was an incredible amount of harassment at Kabul University. Unmarked cars were constantly unloading men without badges who would drag professors off campus. Once, they dragged a professor away in the middle of his lecture, in front of his students. There was no subtlety. There was no attempt at subtlety. None were ever seen again.

With my employment at Kabul University, I received a local passport. This allowed me travel around the country. I left for Herat immediately, having grown a mustache. I had to grow one, to show allegiance to the regime. My mustache opened all of the checkpoints on the new road to Herat, through Kandahar. But my mustache did not place me above suspicion to the intelligence agencies. I was being followed everywhere I went.

When I reached Herat, bombed to oblivion, I was speechless. It was a ghost town. There was nobody on the streets. No shops were open. The few faces you saw carried solemn expressions. Nobody talked to anybody as they passed each other. I took a horse-drawn rickshaw down a street called Copper Street. The street was well known in Herat for being noisy at all hours, full of blacksmiths hammering pots and pans into shape. The only sound was the horses' hooves on the dirt road, pulling my carriage.

My son opened the door when I knocked at our family house, and I rushed inside to find the rest of my family safe and secure. I was overcome with emotion. I held them all tightly and did not want to let go. My entire family was safe. Against all odds, they had survived the bombing that killed so many of our friends and neighbors. My older brother had not been as fortunate. A Soviet bomb fell on his house and killed his entire family. Together, we mourned the loss of his wife and children.

After two days with my family, I decided to return to Kabul for their safety. I had been told that security agents from KHAD, the state intelligence service, were after me, looking for an excuse to arrest me. I went back to Kabul to prove to the authorities I had nothing to hide. That I was here only to teach.

In actuality, I had by this time resolved to leave the country with my family. I worked on my plan while teaching at Kabul University, which was getting worse day by day. More rallies. More professors being dragged away. More students pushing for more revolution. More clashes with the fundamentalists. The intellectual space for me and others in the middle had gone.

After several weeks, I returned to Herat. I used the same local passport, subtly changing the authorized dates of travel. They had been written sloppily, and were easy to change. My uncle in Herat had found a reliable Baluch man to take me to Iran. The Baluch tribes live on both sides of the boundaries of Afghanistan and Iran, as well as Afghanistan and Pakistan. They move freely, ignoring those modern, political demarcations and following ancient tribal paths known only to them.

One of the few things I had brought back to Afghanistan with me was a letter from the chairman of the department of English at the University of Arizona. This letter invited me to come to the university as a visiting scholar. I decided I would take this letter to Tehran, to the US Embassy there, and then go back to the US. It was too dangerous to stay in Afghanistan another day.

Crossing Into Iran

He was very young, the boy who took me across the Afghan border into Iran.

We used his motorcycle for the first part of the trip, and left when the sun began rising. We drove out into the desert, with nothing but sand in any direction. It was incredibly hot. Eventually, we came across a tent. He told me to get into the tent and wait for his return. An enormous Afghan shepherd dog was my only company. The dog could not make a decision whether to attack or protect me, and kept looking at me. It didn't trust me. In the early evening he returned, and we made our way to his village, only a handful of miles from the Iranian border. He opened the gate to his family house, told me to go in, and again sped off.

I walked into the yard and stood there. At that point I still had my mustache, which had again helped me travel unmolested from Kabul to Herat via Kandahar. The young man's father eventually came out of the house, and found me standing in his yard. He was incredibly tall, with dark, leather-like skin, and was wearing a tightly wrapped turban around his head. He looked furious. He asked me to go inside, and pointed not at his house but at his stable, where he kept his animals. I was horrified, and wondered to myself what was happening. In Afghan culture, or any other culture I would imagine, being told to go stay with the animals while a guest is highly offensive.

The young man with the motorcycle eventually returned, and asked his father where their guest was. His father dismissively told him that his damn Communist guest was in the barn with the other animals. His son cried out that I was not a Communist, and that my mustache was just a cover. He said I was an honored guest who knew the mujahideen. Though that was not true, his father came to the stable and begged for forgiveness on his knees. He even tried to kiss my hand. He then produced a letter from his pocket, and asked me to read it to him, as the entire family was illiterate. I read the letter aloud. It was from a mujahideen group aligned with Burhanuddin Rabbani, who would eventually become an interim president of the country for a month in 2001 after the fall of the Taliban, and later assassinated by the Taliban. Hearing this letter, the father became very emotional, and thanked me endlessly for reading it to him. He arranged a sumptuous dinner.

Two days later, in the evening, my young guide and I crossed the Iranian border. We wore all white garments, and walked for many kilometers on our hands and knees. We had to look like sheep to the Iranian guards patrolling the border. The Iranian guards welcomed sheep, because they could kill the sheep for dinner, but Afghans would be shot on sight. My knees were cut in a thousand places. My hands were ripped and bloodied almost immediately. On we went, for hours, in the darkness, the whistling wind the only sound. I was exhausted.

We reached a highway, and waited for several hours until we were sure no cars were around, and then crossed it. After a few more kilometers of hiking, we found his ancestral village and home, and I collapsed into bed.

The next morning, back on a motorcycle, another Baluch tribesman took me to Mashad, a major city in northeast Iran. He helped me find a place to live through his tribal network, and by the evening I had settled into a small room above a market near the center of town. That afternoon, I decided to report to one of the newly created revolutionary committees. I was going to tell them that I had crossed their border illegally but hoped to stay to teach and work, and that I had a PhD. My plan was to await the arrival of my family, obtain a local passport, save funds, and eventually leave. I wore the only suit I had packed.

On my way to the government offices, I saw a demonstration.

I was moving opposite the direction of the demonstrators, and did my best to avoid them. I took a side street, and ran into a group going to join the demonstration. They surrounded me and asked if I would go with them. I said I was busy and had other things to do. They insisted. I told them I was not even Iranian, that I was Afghan, and had no say in these matters. They asked if I were Muslim. They knew that nobody could say no to this question in a nation full of Muslims. I said of course I am Muslim. So I joined them, but left the protestors after traveling only one city block.

And in just those few minutes I began to see just how much Iran had changed, now the victim of its own Islamic revolution that had occurred just months earlier. The parallels with Afghanistan were unnerving. The same fanaticism. The same willingness, even eagerness, to use violence for political gain. The same destruction of the individual in preference for mass, populist action. The same look in their eyes as the extremists, the distant look of a true believer.

It was what I had worked so hard to leave behind in Afghanistan. I had escaped Communism only to fall into the fire of revolutionary Iran.

By the 1970s, major changes were sweeping the Muslim world, most of which would bring a new, highly politicized version of Islam to the forefront of everyday life. From the 1940s and 1950s, monarchies had been ended, replaced by secularists who hoped to modernize their countries. By the end of the 1970s, these secularists would in turn have to give power, and in some cases their lives, to growing demands for Islamic leadership. Nowhere was this more true than in Shah Mohammad Reza Pahlavi's Iran.

The Shah of Iran, more than a monarch, was a complicated figure. Quick to use force to stifle any threats to his absolute power, he also spent lavishly on programs designed to quickly modernize the Iranian state. Using funds from a treasury brimming with petrodollars, he launched a series of focused programs that concentrated on education, modernizing the military, and women's rights. He invested massively in infrastructure, creating Iran's highway network and bringing electricity to large swathes of the country. He readily accepted and recognized Israel, and sought strong trade ties. Iran officially pursued a path of non-alliance throughout the Cold War but as the Shah was a staunch anti-Communist, he sought a close relationship with the United States. By the mid 1960s, Iran became the largest recipient of foreign aid from the United States outside of NATO, and thousands of US businessmen and government advisors were living in the country.

Nonetheless, by the late 1970s, both liberals and conservatives in Iran agreed that things had gone terribly wrong. Conservatives were angered by what they saw as Western cultural influence pervading their country. Liberals were furious with a repressive state intelligence agency that acted with impunity and allowed no room for debate or dissent. And so they joined forces under one banner, the lowest common denominator they could all agree on: Islam.

The man they chose to lead them to a better life was a cleric named Ruhollah Khomeini, an ayatollah and an outspoken critic of the Shah's regime who had been repeatedly arrested and eventually exiled to Paris in 1964. Though he would not return to Iran until the Shah abdicated his throne in 1979, through a series of cassette tapes and letters widely distributed by his loyal followers, he would emerge as the key opposition leader by the mid 1970s. With his consistent and unrelenting message that the Shah was attacking the very roots of Islam and Islamic identity in Iran, Khomeini created the ideological space for all those who thought Iran was going in the wrong direction. He tapped into powerful religious undercurrents in the overwhelmingly Muslim country.

Protests, many of them deadly, against the Shah reached their apogee in late 1978, and in January of 1979 the Shah and his wife left Iran forever. Khomeini returned from France the next month to a crowd of millions of Iranians singing the praises of Islam and Khomeini, saying they would follow both forever. Khomeini's use of religion as a political weapon had worked, and he immediately created the structure for a theocracy with himself at the top, alone interpreting and divining God's will. To be a good Shia Muslim and to be a good citizen of Iran now meant the same thing: complete obedience to Khomeini and his government. Being a Muslim had previously meant being a modest and trustworthy person who prayed daily for grace. This was all replaced. Their slogans, visible everywhere, were the best summaries of what they wanted. "A Good Muslim Is A Revolutionary Muslim. A Good Muslim Is Ready To Sacrifice Himself For The Islamic Government."

And so with reactionary Communism in Afghanistan, so too with revolutionary Islam in Iran. The first thing on the agenda in both countries was to purify the nation of undesirable elements through violence.

Into this fiery, post-revolutionary Iran I arrived in June, 1979. Disappearing quickly was the nation I knew for its astonishing and irreplaceable contributions to literature and poetry. Gone was the beautiful harmony and grace of a proud country with staggering history stretching back more than 5,000 years. Leaving were large swathes of its tolerant and diverse population. Leaving were the foreigners and the intellectuals, even those who had quietly supported the revolution. I would eventually join them.

I learned much about the rules of the new, blood-soaked Iran from my first encounter with a revolutionary committee in charge of Mashad's security. Everyone there was young, and the room was full of slogans praising the sacrifice of individuals who had died in the revolution. Their faces were everywhere, on posters plastered on every open space. This really unnerved me, staring at the faces of so many dead men. I had been in Iran for less than 24 hours.

Before they asked where I had come from, or what business I had with their committee, they asked if I were Muslim. I learned that this was now the primary prism through which the ruling examined the ruled in Iran: religion. Then they asked a series of indirect questions, trying to figure out who I was. I said you don't have to be so indirect, you can tell from my name alone that I am a Sunni Muslim from a Tajik background, maybe from Afghanistan. They asked if I were Shia. I again said that from my name alone you know that I am Sunni. They took this under consideration. They asked where I was from, and what I was doing in Iran. I told them I wanted a local passport to go to Tehran, now needed to travel anywhere inside Iran, just as in Communist Afghanistan and the Soviet Union. Learning about my PhD, they said they wanted me first to go to Mashad University, then still known as Ferdowsi University after the great poet. They said I should ask the president of the university if he needs any professors. The committee told me that they knew he did not have any professors to teach English, as all the foreign English professors had left. I said I would much prefer to receive a local passport to travel to Tehran. Lowering his voice and speaking softly, one of the committee members said it would be better for me to go talk to the university president first. Otherwise, there may be problems. I got the hint.

Ferdowsi University had a reputation at that time as one of the best universities in Iran. I met the president, and the first thing he told me was that Ferdowsi University had an academic partnership with Georgetown University in the United States. This short man, a medical doctor, was very proud of this. But with a heavy, hushed voice, he said that all but a few of his foreign professors had left, and that he did not have enough English professors. I told him that I wanted to travel to Tehran to get a passport and leave to the United States. He smiled at this, and told me everyone would like to do the same. But he begged me to stay and teach for a short while, until the situation improved, and then he would do everything he could to help me travel safely. I reluctantly agreed, realizing the unlikelihood of being issued a visa to leave Iran while the country was in such turmoil. The US-Iran hostage crisis would soon make it impossible to get a visa at the US Embassy.

My boss, the chairman of the English department, was a humorous man who had received his PhD from a university in Texas. He was openly critical of the regime, routinely cursing them right in front of me, and also at our first meeting. He was married to an American woman, and his father was a famous poet. Eventually he would leave as well, returning to Texas, but for now he was my boss.

I began teaching English. I quickly realized that universities were one of the most dangerous places to work in this new country, because the only resistance remaining to the new government were organized students. The government aggressively hunted these students.

In Afghanistan, I had watched my colleagues at Kabul University, the professors and lecturers, be dragged away and killed by the Communists. Now, with a heavy heart that felt every execution, I watched my student body at this Iranian university dwindle.

I absolutely dreaded roll call in the mornings. I wished somebody would come and take me away to be executed rather than learning of yet another bright student deemed a counter-revolutionary and kidnapped and executed all in the same night. I would arrive in the classroom, take a deep breath, and make my way through the names. The students always knew immediately who was missing, and if I looked out over the desks before the call, I too could learn. But I never did. I wasn't sure I could keep my composure at the sight of an empty desk, inhabited just the previous day by a beautiful and curious young man or woman. I kept the list close to my face and read through the names as calmly as I could, putting a little tick mark next to whoever was missing. Sometimes, thankfully, a student would genuinely be sick and miss a class or two. More often, however, I would call out a name and the air would become heavy with foreboding. The silence would be unbearable. My heart would be wrenched into pieces. I would look up, just over the edge of the roll call list, and see a classroom full of students, sullen expressions on their faces, staring at the floor. I would finish the roll call and teach the class, and one or two students would come up to me at the end of the lecture and whisper quietly that the owner of the female name I had called had been executed last night, or the male I called had been missing since the weekend, and they were expecting the worst.

With the help of the university president, my wife and family eventually came to join me, legally, in Mashad. This brought me tremendous joy. I moved out of my small apartment near the market and into a bigger apartment on the other side of town. As we spent the first night together, we were woken up by loud sounds at midnight. I had moved right next to a military base, and at midnight most nights, they executed suspected counter-revolutionaries. They executed my students. I would go to teach my classes the next day, and if there were missing students, I would realize that I had heard their deaths the night before. I could not breath that first night. I never slept well in all my time in Mashad, worried, as night approached, that one my students would be among the group being lined up and gunned down in the name of purifying the country.

All of these experiences amounted to a hard lesson about life in the new Iran: you are not allowed to be yourself. You must be a member of the flock. You are not allowed to keep your individuality. The tools to implement this ranged from mandatory dress codes for women to execution of all people who spoke out against injustice. You had to lie to yourself. You had to lie to your friends, you had to lie to society. You had to live a double life, and this brings a lot of guilt. To this day, to a certain extent, this is still true in Iran.

My struggle during my time in Iran was to retain my individuality. To not be a party member, an Islamist, a revolutionary, a fanatic. To be myself, to retain my own freedom, and to stay alive. This was difficult because you were forced to live with multiple personalities. You were only yourself with your family. It was difficult to trust friends. Difficult to trust neighbors. Difficult to trust students. Everybody thought everybody was spying on each other. And I always thought the whole thing cannot be real. No society can function like this, with everybody lying to each other.

Khomeini, after my second year of work and his second year in power, apparently concluded that executing all of the students opposed to his regime might not actually be possible. He opted to instead simply close all of the universities. As he understood it, all of the universities were hopelessly under the control of dissident groups like the Mujahideen e Khalq, or People's Mujahideen. To some extent, he may have been correct. University campuses across the country were incredibly active. They were fertile grounds for young Communists, young Islamic Communists, young monarchists, young secularists and other groups looking for a say in the ruling of the country. Many of these groups had underground newspapers and published frequently.

One night, I received a knock on the door of my house. I opened the door to find a group of young women, students of mine, standing in the doorway. I invited them in, and they told me that they were being hunted by the new state intelligence agency, which bore remarkable similarities to the last state intelligence agency. Members of a resistance group, they could not go home, and their only other friends had been arrested, so they decided to go to my house.

At that time, Khomeini had issued another ruling, saying that anybody caught harboring members of resistance groups would be executed alongside their guests.

My wife and I quickly put them in the basement, and fed and clothed them for some time. I did not know which specific group they were from, I knew only that I was unable to shut the door on a group of people who desperately needed my help. After several days, they left, forever grateful. My wife and I breathed more easily. We had put our entire family at incredible risk.

I had tried, briefly, not to be sympathetic to these young people and the passion with which they argued and fought for a better, more inclusive Iran. I had tried to stay neutral. But the brutal manner in which they were hunted and executed by the Islamic regime made it impossible. A basic level of humanity never escaped me.

With universities closing, I was asked to move from teaching to translation. This was the only thing left for academics in Iran to do other than mindless research that was rarely published.

I was asked to translate a book by Dr. Ali Shariati. Shariati was an Iranian dissident, writer, scholar and philosopher who had received his doctorate from Sorbonne University in France. He had written several books about how Shia Islam could be updated and modernized, and was a fierce critic of the Shah. He was a very popular figure, widely read in Iran and Afghanistan, and a brilliant thinker. He died before the revolution took place, and rumors swirl to this day about an assassination by the Shah's police.

Even though he supported the revolution, it is unlikely he would have supported the violence used after the revolution succeeded. This is why I was surprised when I was handed an uncensored version of his book, which contained a famous chapter comparing two kinds of Shia Islam. The first, Shariati argued, was a more just, humble, innocent and historical Shiism, which emerged as a reaction against injustice. He compared this to a politicized and ritualistic Shiism that emerged in the Safavid period of Iranian history, where Shia Islam was manipulated not in the interest of the people, but for the clerical establishment. He said the latter was highly dangerous. And anybody who read his words could easily see that this described perfectly Khomeini's new religious government. Shia Islam had been masterfully manipulated for the benefit of the clerics, who had felt marginalized under the Shah. These clerics were now running the country.

With mullahs as politicians, the role of the mosque changed. The mosque as I understood it was a place only for prayer, five times a day. It was considered an affront to God to even discuss politics in a mosque when I was a child. But in Iran, mosques had birthed a revolution, and so now had a different function: they served as sustainers of the revolution. It was a place to discuss politics. It was a place to discuss the latest martyrs and see their pictures. It was a place to discuss the war with Iraq. It was a place to listen to the clerics spread fear. In mosques I heard clerics urging people to report counter-revolutionaries to the government and spreading accusations against this or that minority religious sect. They screamed the names of individuals deemed not Islamic enough. The mosque had lost its mission. Those loudspeakers overhead amplified a message of hate and fear.

I worried about the danger of translating this article, but when I was finished I handed it back up the chain of command. Nobody said anything. The book was eventually published by Ferdowsi University Press, and shipped in large numbers around Iran and around the Muslim world.

My second encounter with the Revolutionary Guards was because of this book. They read it, and one day several came storming into to my office. They demanded to know why I had translated this particular version of the book, the uncensored version. I replied calmly that this was the version I had been handed, and that this project had the support of the president of the university. They yelled at me for betraying the revolution, but, finding no real cause, let me off the hook.

I later learned that the president of the university was a fan of Shariati's philosophy, and had quietly pushed this book to print as his small act of rebellion. The fact that it was dangerous to publish the work of Shariati, who had supported the revolution, showed that the revolution was moving into a new phase. A more dangerous and violent phase. Opposition groups began distributing a graphic with two images of Khomeini, one in black and one in red. The red showed him as a revolutionary, which people had carried against the Shah. The black was supposed to show that he was moving the revolution into darker and more violent areas.

As if demanding I atone for my sins, the Revolutionary Guards soon handed me another book to translate. The author was a very conservative cleric and a former dean of the school of theology at Tehran University. These soldiers appeared to thoroughly enjoy his work and his sermons. I accepted the book from them and took it home with me. I read the first chapter and put it down, telling myself I would never translate this. It was strongly critical of a great Iranian poet named Ahmad Shamloo. He was one of the most popular modern Iranian poets. It was also full of strong language that appeared to condone the use of violence.

I made excuse after excuse, starting by saying that the book contained poetry, which is almost impossible to translate well. They said that another book I had translated had contained poetry. I appealed to their ego, saying the book had such powerful ideas I was unsure how to effectively write them in another language. They accused me of stalling. They checked in with me every day, asking how many pages I had translated and how much longer it would take. I would sometimes translate just a few paragraphs to temporarily feed their appetite.

They eventually realized I was playing with them, and responded by expelling my son from school. He was in the third grade. I don't think they knew they had handed me a gift. My son had never gotten along well with Iranian students, and I had never wanted my son to be in these schools. The Iranian students, even in the third grade, would always try to force him to pray against his will. To drag him to the mosque. His teacher, who adored him, called him a brilliant rebel and troublemaker. I smiled when I heard this, and enrolled him in an English language program. The rest of his studies I taught him myself.

The last phase of my life in Iran began when the Revolutionary Guards accused me of having links to opposition groups, some of whom violently resisted the new government. They argued that because a friend of mine was a member of an opposition group, I must be too. I told them that I had never known this academic friend was a member of anything, and that I certainly wasn't. They eventually arrested him and increasingly put pressure on me to admit that I had ties to violent groups. I had no ties to such groups.

Their increasing paranoia also became evident. In one meeting with them, the day after they had arrested my friend, they accused me of simultaneously working for the Afghan Communist government, the Afghan resistance against that government, the Soviet government, the KGB and the CIA. I couldn't stifle my laugh, which infuriated them. I told them they had to pick one of them first, and then I could tell them that I had no ties to that group. I told them that everything they were accusing me of was based on paranoia, which they did not enjoy hearing.

After that meeting, my friend's sister got in contact with me. She told me that my friend had overheard my name while being arrested, and he told his sister to urge me to leave Mashad as soon as possible. By the next day I was on a bus to Tehran with my family, having received my local passport after completing my first book translation. My friends in Mashad complied with my last request, which was to tell the authorities, if asked, that they thought I was headed to Pakistan.

The first night in Tehran nearly resulted in the death of me and my entire family. Khomeini's agents, increasingly focused on national defense as the war with Iraq dragged into its fourth year, had partially relented on hunting down opposition groups. The Mujahideen e Khalq, taking advantage of this window, exploded an enormous car bomb, parked near the hotel we had wanted to check into. Though welcomed into the hotel initially, when the staff discovered we were Afghans, we were asked abruptly to leave. As we approached another hotel a few blocks away, the car bomb exploded, blowing off the entire front of the hotel, killing dozens and shattering windows half a kilometer away.

The Iran-Iraq War, which had seemed somewhat distant in Mashad, was in full swing in Tehran. Iraq frequently bombed the city. The war alarm, that piercing warning that death was flying fast overhead in my direction, sounded almost every night. And so when the Iraqi bombers flew over Tehran, we made our way to whatever basement was nearby. It also sounded at random times during the day. When it happened during the day, you could see thousands of panicked people running towards any building, picking up children and dropping their groceries. The streets would empty in minutes. And inside those buildings we would await the horrible sounds of death. It is a sickening sensation, to listen for the sounds of explosions which you understand means people are dying. To understand that lives are being extinguished. The only sound worse than an explosion was the silence of a room full of men, women and children holding their breaths, praying silently to be spared. You never knew whether your turn to die had arrived.

The war, started by an opportunistic Saddam Hussein on September 22, 1980, would carry on for eight years and result in the deaths of more than a million people, the majority of which were Iranian. It had incalculable effects on the new regime, which radicalized even further in the face of an existential threat. It turned their already radical Shiism into a cult that glorified death and martyrdom. The Iraqis had attacked first, hoping to solve the problem of an ancient disputed border territory by taking advantage of the relative chaos of the revolution in Iran. They then defended against the Iranians, who in turn would then defend against the Iraqis, and so on for the better part of a decade. It resembled World War I, replete with bayonet charges, trench warfare, human wave charges, and even the use of mustard gas and sarin nerve gas, which had been provided to Iraq by Germany during the war.

Iran came to resemble a funeral procession. You could see the faces of martyrs of the war everywhere, frequently updated with latest pictures of the dead. Every street name was changed to honor another dead young man. The prices of food products skyrocketed. Meat was available at stores only twice a week. The nation, so rich in natural gas and oil, was forced to ration it to its citizens. They stood in unending lines that snaked around multiple city blocks.

The word Islamic was applied to everything. The word revolutionary was applied to everything. Islamic soap. Islamic detergent. They even started producing Islamic Coca-Cola.

We moved hotels frequently, wanting to stay off the radar of the Revolutionary Guard, who may have figured out that I was actually still in Iran. My first visit in Tehran was to the offices of the United Nations Development Program (UNDP), where a very nice Indian man reviewed my documents and told me I was indeed eligible for political asylum in the US. I eagerly filled out all the required forms, and he sent them on to the US Embassy in Rome, Italy. The next problem was that I did not have a passport, which was still sitting in Kabul in one of the Afghan ministries. I could get a visa from the Italian Embassy, but I needed a passport. Fortunately, this nice Indian man at UNDP passed my case on to the Red Cross, who used their connections in the Iranian government to find me a way out of the country. The Red Cross prepared the paperwork for me to be deported me to Italy. I wish I could have kept that last piece of paper, which I smiled broadly as I signed. An unforgettable header ran across the top of the page. An Undesirable Element To Be Deported As Soon As Possible.

Though translating Shariati's book had gotten me into trouble in Mashad, it proved helpful in Tehran. On one of my last days in Iran, I went to the Central Bank to convert my Iranian rials into US dollars. I had what I calculated as about $400 in rials. The teller on the other side of the desk, on seeing my signature, asked me if I was the Sharif Fayez who had translated Shariati's book. Seeing his necktie, which indicated a liberal attitude and perhaps an old allegiance to the Shah, I said I was. He smiled broadly and said that he was a devoted student of Shariati's work, and had met him several times before his death. He asked me for my opinions on some of the finer points of Shariati's philosophy, which we discussed at length in hushed voices. Eventually, he gave me my converted currency. I was shocked when he handed me exactly $5,000, more than ten times the value of what I had given him to convert. Before I could say anything, he urged me on my way, and smiled again as he said he was more than happy to help out a friend. When I eventually landed in the US, this money would allow me a cushion with which to set up my new life.

On the plane, the mood was one of exuberance. Many other passengers on the plane were people like me. Undesirable elements. The minute the plane took off, bound for Rome, every woman took off her headscarf, no longer required by law to wear it. The men all smiled. Everyone was now able to decide what being a Muslim meant to them.

The plane landed in Rome. Several passengers kissed the ground as they exited the plane. We were safe. We were free.

The Italian Red Cross met us at the airport and took us to our hotel in Rome. We stayed for several nights in Rome, embracing an aura of peace and tranquility. Eventually, the Italian Red Cross moved us to Ladispoli, a beach city in central Italy. Expensive during the summers, it was all but abandoned when we lived there in the fall and early winter.

Every afternoon I would take our kids to the beach, and we would walk and watch the sunset. My beautiful daughter Nadia would pick flower petals from along the beach and put them in my pocket when I wasn't watching. I felt an indescribable calm permeate my soul. I felt I could recover my life, long dormant and buried under layers of fear and lies. At long last, I felt alive.

The US Embassy began processing our applications. My old friend Cecil Robinson was now the chair of the English Department at the University of Arizona in Tucson. He eagerly agreed to sponsor my family in the United States. After several interviews with the US Embassy, we left for the United States.

I spent several years at the University of Arizona in Tucson working as a translator, as a research assistant, and occasionally teaching. They had a large oriental studies library, which fascinated me. I spent much of my free time reading obscure texts from around the world.

My children perfectly adjusted to their new lives, as did my wife. Life was going very well.

The pace of my life slowed down considerably, but this never bothered me. I never forgot my life in Afghanistan and Iran. I never forgot colleagues and friends who were still stuck in those countries, surviving as best they could. I woke up each day amazed that I was alive and free to do whatever I wanted.

After several years, I moved with my family to Virginia. There were several translation companies there that I began working for.

When I wasn't translating, I was writing about the situation in Afghanistan. I watched from a bird's eye view the painful collapse of the country on every level.

THE SOVIET WITHDRAWAL

When the Soviets withdrew on February 15, 1989, it was a truly great day for all of us. The Afghans in the United States held parties and celebrated, and prayed. We had been eagerly awaiting this day from April 15, 1988, when the Soviet government signed the Geneva Accords, which laid out a detailed plan for a phased withdrawal for Soviet troops from Afghanistan. It also provided pledges of non-interference by the United States and the Soviet Union, and led to Afghanistan and Pakistan signing several agreements.

The war had taken an astonishing toll on the country. One million dead Afghans. One million disabled Afghans. Three million maimed or wounded, primarily civilians. Half of the arable land and livestock in the country destroyed, irrigation systems bombed to oblivion. Kandahar, Afghanistan's second largest city, went from a population of 200,000 to 25,000 in just eight years. More than 10 million land mines were planted, which Red Cross estimated would take 4,000 years without interruption to remove. More than half of the children in the country were malnourished, lacking access to food. That famous statistic about Afghan refugees became a reality because of this war: By the 1980s, half of all refugees in the world were Afghan. Between five and ten million people fled the country to Pakistan and Iran, or almost a third of the country. Two million more were displaced inside the country. And yet the numbers, as horrifying as they are, tell not half the story. It is difficult to define and quantify what it means to have the soul of a country destroyed.

MUJAHIDEEN

Impossibly, the greatest tragedy was yet to come. This would be the final straw to break the camel's back. While we celebrated the Soviet withdrawal, in hushed tones we worried, even as far away as the United States, about the future. We all knew the ferocity of the mujahideen groups. Many of us had friends or colleagues who either openly or quietly supported them. I had become close to several members of the Northern Alliance, with a movement run by a man named Ahmad Shah Massoud in particular. We never met, but he and his followers read my work. We knew they were all patriots, but we did not know the storm that was brewing over the horizon. We did not realize to what extent the war had radicalized them, making them beyond dialogue and beyond reconciliation, even with each other. From the day of the Soviet withdrawal in February, 1989, it would be Afghans killing Afghans, fighting over the pieces of a shattered country. We have no one to blame but ourselves.

The earliest warning sign of trouble was the mujahideen opposition to any form of discussion with Mohammad Najibullah, president of the Afghan government during the Soviet withdrawal. He was a wise man and a reasonable person. Najibullah had made insistent and generous offers to the mujahideen to come into the government, to accept a power sharing agreement that would allow them a major voice in the running of the country. He continually showed the proverbial olive branch. The mujahideen adamantly refused to talk to him or recognize his government. Najibullah, even after the Soviet withdrawal, still had a large military at his disposal with an enormous arsenal. They were not irreparably Communist, nor was his government. And the world had watched the Berlin Wall collapse. The world knew Communism was no longer a threat to anyone, that it was collapsing. Afghanistan could have been saved.

With the refusal of the mujahideen to talk with Najibullah, the final destruction of Afghanistan began. Different militant groups began attacking different cities, and new warlords emerged. Each ruled their own fiefdom. The Soviets must be held accountable for their role in destroying the country. But so too must the mujahideen. Kabul, remarkably well intact after a decade of fighting, was completely destroyed not by Soviet soldiers but by Afghan soldiers as they fought for influence. Block by block, each warlord created his own area of control, extorting populations and raising militias.

The mujahideen did eventually establish their own government in 1992, but not without an astonishing amount of bloodshed. Without a single Soviet soldier in the country, Afghans would kill more than 400,000 of their own countrymen in the years after the collapse of the Najibullah government. Our worst fears were realized. Rabbani became president, with a particularly fierce Islamist named Gulbuddin Hekmatyar his prime minister. Several other famous mujahideen members were in this coalition government as well. Remarkably, as they all talked with each other during the day and discussed politics, they went home to their different areas of control around Kabul and rocketed and attacked each other by night. Massoud's base of operations was his fortress-like Panjshir Valley to the north. Hekmatyar launched rockets indiscriminately into Kabul from Logar in the south. Rabbani fought back from areas under his control in Kabul. Ethnic factions began coalescing and attacking other ethnic groups, completely independent of the mujahideen. Pakistan, flagrantly violating the agreements it had signed in Geneva, continued arming its favorite groups, cheering them on to ever greater destruction. The US, checked out of the war after the withdrawal of the Soviets, left Pakistan to do what it wanted. Kabul descended into hell.

I became permanently disillusioned with the mujahideen I had vocally supported against the Soviets while watching their rise to power and their interactions with the Najibullah government. Most of the leaders knew who I was. They knew I had never wavered in my commitment to an Afghanistan free of Communist and Soviet interference.

My brother, who had left Afghanistan and gone to the Soviet Union to study in its universities in the 1980s, was looking to escape and join me in the United States. Even though it was 1991, the Soviet Union had not yet collapsed and travel restrictions were severe. It was not easy to leave, particularly to Europe. I recommended he travel first to Peshawar, in Pakistan, where

I could help him using my contacts and friends in the US government. He could travel to the edges of the Soviet Union, and then onwards into Pakistan.

He eventually arrived in Pakistan, but after several weeks went missing and I stopped hearing from him. I grew concerned. I went to Peshawar to look for him. It was very easy for me, using contacts in the US and Afghanistan, to locate several different groups and talk with them about my brother. The commanders all welcomed me. Even Hekmatyar's group, which I never liked and had nothing in common with, met with me and discussed the fate of my brother. All of the commanders said that while they didn't know where he was, they would investigate.

I left after a week, needing to be back in the US for several conferences. I continued gathering information, and quickly returned to Pakistan. This time I discovered where he was, though I would not be allowed to see him until he was released. The circumstances of his arrest gave a glimpse into the future.

He had been arrested by a hardline element inside Rabbani's group. His arrest was unknown even to Rabbani at the time. He had been arrested because he had US dollars in his pocket. This was amazing to me because all of these groups had received millions of US dollars directly from the US government to fight against the Soviets. The guns they used were supplied by the US. The rockets they had launched were supplied by the US. The priceless logistical support they had been given was from the US. They either didn't know this or didn't care. They said that because he had US dollars in his pocket, he was one of their spies, and they were threatening to kill him.

Despite everything the US had done for these groups, arming them and supporting them in their fight, it had not bought an ounce of goodwill. Most of them resented the US even as it armed them. Even as President Reagan hosted some of them at the White House and lauded them as freedom fighters. The double sided relationship of the US's relationship with these groups was becoming clear to me.

I told the group that I had sent him the money, which he was to use to travel and join me in the United States. I told them that having US dollars was a ridiculously stupid way to determine who was a spy. And I told them they had two weeks to release my brother, or their would be consequences. He was being held in an underground prison run by Rabbani's group in Pakistan near the Afghan border. They released him on the condition he never tell anyone about where he had been or what he had seen. He of course told me everything the minute we left the country. All of the atrocities he had seen. I had always known most of what he told me. But being so close to it made it hard to place in the grander scheme of war and all the pain and sorrow war brings. My concern about what these groups would do in the future, if they were so quick to use violence against each other and Afghan civilians, grew. Some were remarkably less violent and corrupt than others, particularly Massoud's group based out of Panjshir. But infighting would plague them all and almost irrevocably destroy Afghanistan.

Taliban

On September 27, 1996, after several years oscillating between mujahideen rule and lawlessness, a group of madrassah teachers and mujahideen commanders collectively known as the Taliban took control of Kabul. It was the culmination of a two year effort that had begun in Kandahar and made its way across the country. The atrocities of this group against minorities, against women, and against the very roots of civilization itself have been well documented. While their rise to power may have had logical roots, working to restore law and order in a country devoid of both, their rule once in power was the most savage and inhumane the world had seen in centuries. Despite being recognized only by their sponsor state Pakistan, which they could not live without, the United Arab Emirates and Saudi Arabia, their fanaticism was world famous.

It was interesting to watch the reactions of Afghans living in the United States to this new group. They ranged considerably, sometimes following ethnic lines and sometimes following what people thought was good for the country. Some argued passionately that they should be allowed to take the entire country so that at least Afghanistan would be under the rule of one group that could then be talked to, instead of under many groups. They said that the Taliban can unify the entire country. Others argued that this group must be defeated, motived as tales of their treatment of women and minority groups spread. They argued the opposition groups, including Massoud's group in the Northern Alliance, should be strengthened. They knew that the Taliban could not be moderated. And the last group were happy with the Taliban. I was always surprised by how many Taliban supporters there were among the Afghan-American community in the United States, particularly in Washington, DC.

There was no consensus. The Afghan diaspora was confused about what to do. The differences reached into religion, with some mosques in Virginia being pro-Taliban and some being anti-Taliban. Taliban representatives, who, astonishingly, traveled quite freely, often came to pray at mosques and raise awareness and money.

But most Afghans had, despite only recently arriving in their new countries, sadly left Afghanistan behind them for good. Now, they were only casual observers, at a time when their country desperately needed their help.

Even the Voice of America, a radio program in Afghanistan, spoke with two voices. Their Pashtu programs were sympathetic to the Taliban, and their Dari program was hostile to the Taliban. A group of us, Afghans still checked into Afghanistan, often talked about this, trying to determine if this was US policy. We realized eventually that Voice of America had lost control of its program, with the Pashtuns in the Pashtu language segment saying one thing, and the Dari speaking minorities in the Dari segment saying another thing.

There was also a pro-Taliban radio station in California, which regularly promoted Taliban views. Taliban representatives would come to California and be given glowing radio interviews. They would also come to Washington, DC, and meet with US government officials.

While the Afghan diaspora discussed the Taliban issue passionately from afar, Massoud himself went to meet this new group before they took Kabul. He went to them alone and unarmed, and hoped to convince them to work with him to bring stability to the country. From his post as defense minister for the mujahideen government, he asked them to help him hold a democratic election process for a new government. They refused. He returned to Kabul. The Taliban leader who met Massoud was executed by more senior Taliban leaders for failing to kill Massoud when he had had a chance. This story, combined with others about the Taliban's uneducated leader, Mullah Omar, led me to conclude that those who hoped the Taliban could be civilized and reasoned with were severely misguided. They were neither civil nor reasonable people.

I began writing more articles against the Taliban. My friends and I tried to lobby Congress against dealing with the group, knowing that the US government occasionally had contact with the Taliban either directly or through Pakistani intermediaries. We held demonstrations in front of the Capitol building. Our purpose was to highlight the danger of bestowing any international legitimacy to this group. Eventually, the Taliban would appoint a representative to the UN, who lived in New York City and Washington, DC. He was well known to the Afghan-American community, and occasionally commented on what was happening in the country.

Much as I wanted, I was unable to bring myself to attempt to discuss with him what his group was doing to my beloved country. I was not interested in hearing someone attempt to explain the rationale behind their public executions and massacres of women and minorities. I was not interested in hearing a defense of why schools and universities had to be closed. I was not interested in their exclusively ethnic Pashtun nationalism, pursued at the expense of Afghanistan's diverse ethnic heritage. I was not interested in hearing why the burqa had become mandatory for women. I did not find admirable the group's need for the production and sale of opium. I resented the group's dependence on Pakistan for money, guns and illiterate foot-soldiers, something that should have been regarded as treason to any true Afghan.

My friends and I cheered when President Clinton signed executive order 13129 into effect on July 6, 1999. This officially banned trade with Taliban regime, and froze assets the government had stashed abroad. We were thrilled when the UN that same year banned all international flights of their Afghan airline, Ariana, which the Taliban used to bring guns into the country and opium out. We were overcome with joy when the UN subsequently passed Resolution 1333, which called for all UN member states to close any offices belonging to the Taliban.
The world had seen the Taliban's true colors.

For Afghanistan, 9/11 changed everything. A month after those horrible attacks, special forces soldiers from the US military and other nations were linking up with opposition groups in the mountains of northern Afghanistan and driving the Taliban out of power.

The militant group had become even more extreme in its last year, changing its views as its situation economically and politically deteriorated and rabid Pakistani and Arab jihadists began rising in influence. The famed Buddhas of Bamiyan provide a perfect example.

Mullah Omar himself had issued a statement in 1996 saying that the enormous buddhas of Bamiyan, among other priceless artifacts, should be left alone. He argued that in the future they could be used to promote tourism to Afghanistan, and that since Afghanistan had no Buddhists left, there was no danger of anybody worshipping them. As late as the year 2000, Taliban in Bamiyan had even asked for UN assistance to build ditches to divert rainwater away from the Buddhas to prevent them from deteriorating further. Located at an elevation of 8,000 feet, built in the sixth century and reaching one hundred and twenty and one hundred and eighty feet respectively, the two ancient statues were truly unique. They had survived countless marauding armies for over a millennium, including Genghis Khan. But they would not survive the Taliban. By 2001, the decision had been made to destroy all statues in the country. The Buddhas, along with countless other priceless artifacts, were dynamited and blown to pieces, suddenly declared un-Islamic after more than 1,000 years of Islamic rule in Afghanistan.

The government also had been hosting Osama bin Laden and his terrorist group Al-Qaeda for years. While some members of the Taliban government urged Mullah Omar to hand him over to the US to maintain their rule, he repeatedly refused. He was a guest, he explained simply. Closer to the truth was that the Saudi billionaire was bankrolling large sections of the failing Taliban regime. That the Taliban government had ever given sanctuary to a man like Osama bin Laden at all is indicative of their extremism.

As the Taliban government collapsed and retreated into the hills, temporarily stunned and silenced by overwhelming US firepower, Afghans from their homeland and around the globe began convening in Bonn, Germany, for a conference on the future of the country hosted by the United Nations. This conference, held in November 2001, had grand objectives: to create a new Afghan state that would stand the test of time. A state that would renounce violence and focus on rebuilding and reviving an Afghanistan that had been lost in the last two decades of fighting.

While Hamid Karzai would eventually be elected interim president of the country, the process by which he was elected was fascinating. Various groups with substantial differences jockeyed and maneuvered for a say in the new regime, backed wholeheartedly by the West.

There were four political groups: The Rome Process, The Cyprus Group, The Peshawar Group, and The Northern Alliance Group. The Rome Peace Process was led by none other than King Zahir Shah, who had kissed me on my head as a child in elementary school after I had read to him. The royal family of Afghanistan had fled to Italy after their ousting in the 1970s, and established a new life in Rome. They are still there today.

Old and ailing, the King, bearing the title Father of the Nation, nonetheless commanded immense respect. Though he was not present at the meeting in Bonn and did not explicitly call for a return to monarchy, members of his group did. This group was full of people who were diplomats and civil servants who had worked in Afghanistan's government in the 1970s and 1980s. They wanted a steady, experienced hand to lead the country through this delicate time in history. They supported peace talks with the Taliban. Hamid Karzai, though independent, had a long history with members of this group. Some ministers and government cabinet members even today have roots with this group.

Afghanistan's neighbors, not missing a beat, also backed their respective parties for a voice in the ruling of the country. Pakistan had not given up its support for the Taliban as their weapon of choice to rule Afghanistan, and pleaded that so-called moderate Taliban leaders be allowed to participate, a request that was eventually denied. There is no such thing as a moderate Talib.

The Cyprus Group, a group of Iranian-backed exiles, were opposed to the Taliban as well as the monarchy. They were sympathetic to Gulbuddin Hekmatyar, and wanted a greater role for him. He was the jihadi commander who had briefly been the prime minister of Afghanistan in the 1990s. With the rise of the Taliban, he, along with a number of other powerful jihadi figures, fled to Iran, where they were well taken care of.

The Peshawar Group, named after the Pakistani city, was a group of mainly Pashtun politicians who were connected to various mujahideen groups.

Lastly, there was the Northern Alliance group, which was running an active war against the Taliban across the country. Represented by eleven men and women, they were still mourning the loss of Ahmad Shah Massoud, the guerrilla commander from Panjshir, who had been assassinated by a suicide bomber sent by Al-Qaeda just two days before the 9/11 attacks. In early 2001, Massoud had predicted with incredible accuracy that terrorist groups, enjoying the sanctuary provided to them by the Taliban and their Pakistani hosts, were planning large scale attacks against European and American targets. Even though he said this in front of the entire world at a speech in Brussels, he was applauded and ignored.

The Bonn Conference's first order of business was to agree on a plan to create Afghanistan's new government. By the end of the first day, they had all approved the creation of an interim government that would exist for a maximum of six months. A loya jirga, the traditional Afghan meeting of elders, would be called after this time to create a transitional administration to run the country for the next two years. They would also draft a new Constitution for the country to be approved by a second loya jirga.

While that had gone smoothly, tensions rose as the country's leadership and the status of peacekeeping forces were discussed. The Northern Alliance was in favor of an Afghan force to secure Kabul. All the other groups were opposed to this, thinking that it would precipitate the return to the warlordism that had plagued the country a decade earlier. The Rome, Cyprus and Peshawar groups won the debate, voting for an international peacekeeping force to stay in Kabul under the control of the UN.

The Northern Alliance accepted this, but in turn vehemently opposed the return of the monarchy to Afghanistan, which the rest of the groups supported. By the end of the conference, the monarchists had given way to two lesser known candidates, Abdul Sittar Sirat and Hamid Karzai. Hamid Karzai won the vote at the last minute, becoming the interim president. His jihadi background, resistance to both the Soviets and the Taliban, and membership in a powerful Pashtun family ultimately made him a comfortable choice. Twenty nine Cabinet posts were established and filled by the usual process of political jockeying. The Northern Alliance group received about half of the ministerial positions in the interim government, with the Rome group receiving eight positions.

Two weeks later, the UN Security Council approved the deployment of an international peacekeeping force to Kabul, which Britain agreed to lead. Hamid Karzai was inaugurated shortly before the end of the year, in late December.

MY INVOLVEMENT IN BONN

I was not present in Bonn, despite being asked repeatedly to attend by Northern Alliance and independent friends of mine. They wanted me to consider a ministerial post. I told them I would think about it, but reject it if someone with more promise emerged.

I learned I was Afghanistan's new minister of higher education from my wife. I had come home from work and was preparing some tea when my wife welcomed me home with the honorific of minister. I asked her what she was talking about. She said I was a minister in the new Afghan government. I said what could I possibly be minister of? I am not a minister, nobody has called me about this. She shrugged and said a family friend had called from Europe to congratulate me. The phone began ringing as we were talking. It was another friend congratulating me on my new post. I tepidly thanked him, and hung up. The phone rang again, and again. I thought to myself, there must be a mistake.

I learned from the BBC that I was indeed a newly appointed minister in the interim government. Checking their website I saw my name staring back at me on a copy of a declaration the Bonn Conference had submitted to the press. Sharif Fayez, Minister of Higher Education.

The phone rang again, this time a member of the Bonn committee, who simply asked me if I were ready to return to Kabul. I told him that all of this was a big shock, and that I was honored to have even been considered for the position. He repeated his question, and said I had a day to think it over. I said I would return if this is what were necessary for the country. He said it was.

The phone kept ringing as friends from around the world called to convey their excitement at my position. While I was excited by the opportunity of helping build a new government, I was also concerned for my family. We had finally managed to establish a normal, predictable life. I was finally able to spend the time with my son, daughter and wife that they deserved. I was able to watch them grow and develop in a peaceful environment where they were able to pursue their passions without issue. I was enjoying every single minute.

My wife, sensing my concern, told me I had to accept the offer. She said that this was the culmination of my efforts, begun years ago with a pen and paper, to positively affect the direction of my country. I told her that the decision was ultimately up to her. She told me to go.

I accepted the offer, and before I knew it, a CNN camera crew was in front of my house, preparing a report on some of the leaders of the new government. A few days later, my travel plans confirmed, they followed me all the way to Washington, DC's Dulles International Airport. I traveled from there to Paris, where friends of the new Afghan government ensured I was mobbed by European media and important members of the French government. The shift from an obscure person born in an obscure country to a person of immense interest to the Western world was immediate and overwhelming. I found myself in meetings with high level French diplomats and ministers despite having been unknown to the world a mere two weeks prior. I had not returned to Kabul in years, so there was only so much I could say about my plans and hopes for the future.

After several days, I finally boarded a flight from Paris to Delhi, India, where a special plane had been arranged to bring members of the new government into Afghanistan.

I took a deep breath as the plane to Kabul took off. I had an impossible number of thoughts in my head. I closed my eyes, and let myself be pushed into my seat as the plane climbed into the skies.

The Minister of Higher Education

The extent of the devastation, of what the Afghan mujahideen had wrought, became clear when our plane landed. Unable to land at Kabul's international airport because of the destroyed runway, we taxied into Bagram airbase, the largest airbase in the country, originally built by the Soviets. It is located two hours north of Kabul, not far from the Panjshir Valley. From there we went straight to the Ministry of the Interior for the new Cabinet inauguration.

US Ambassador Ryan Crocker, who opened the US Embassy in Kabul on January 17, 2002, likened Kabul in those days to Berlin in 1945, completely and hopelessly annihilated. I saw what he meant.

Driving through the streets brought tears to my eyes. Kabul had become a city of strangers, full of only the people who were unable to escape. The devastation was heartbreaking. There were no roads. There was no electricity. There was no water. The holes left by rockets and bullets covered the entire city. There were very few people out in public, most of them still scared and following the rules the Taliban had forced on them. There were a handful of standing buildings. There were no cars. The grey skies of winter added a particularly gloomy aura to the city. A city that I remembered as lively and vibrant, full of people, was eerily quiet. Our boots crunched loudly in the light snow that had fallen on the hushed city.

A combination of pride and anger swelled. Pride at the beauty of my country. Pride in our staggering history and contributions to the world. Anger at the mujahideen, some of whom I had known well, who had done this to their own people, their own country. Anger at the Taliban for the impossible savagery of their regime.

After the inauguration of the new Cabinet, I was taken to the Intercontinental Hotel. Despite its name, it had no connection to the international hotel chain. The company had cut ties with it decades earlier, but the name had stuck. All of the ministers were put there temporarily, though we would end up staying for almost five months while offices were built for us.

The hotel, like the rest of Afghanistan, had no telephones, no running water, no electricity, and no heat. This made it incredibly hard for people to do their jobs. We ministers had an enormous mandate from the interim government, from the Afghan people, and from the foreign governments supporting us, but were ill equipped to do the large scale projects so desperate to the rehabilitation of the country. The press was constantly interviewing us about our plans for the future, but we didn't even have telephones to call other governments offices for several weeks. The weather was so cold that I asked a friend coming to Kabul to bring me a sleeping bag. I then took the carpet off the floor of the room and put it over me as I slept.

Despite all of this, the optimism in the air was truly tangible. People, from the street to the government, were increasingly excited about the future. The Americans had been extremely successful in flushing out the Taliban. There was optimism that the US could eliminate the Taliban once and for all and protect our country from Pakistan. There was incredible faith in their power to bring peace. There was no corruption, there was no resistance, and the fundamentalists had gone quiet. The country was at peace, liberated from the dark ages.

THE STATE OF HIGHER EDUCATION IN AFGHANISTAN

My first challenge as a minister in the Afghan government was to reassert control over higher education in Afghanistan, and then rebuild the public universities. Because Afghanistan had fractured, each institution was trying to find its own way forward after the fall of the Taliban.

Even though the universities had largely been closed under the Taliban, they were still being run by ideologues who enjoyed the office space. My work with the campus and president of Kabul University showed me the severity of the challenges ahead.

Kabul University was in a horrifying physical state. The entire campus had been destroyed. There was no running water. There was no heating system of any kind. There were no roofs on buildings. There were no window panes. Pipes had been ripped from the walls to be sold in Pakistan. There was not a functional bathroom. On my first visit to the campus, several journalists from Western newspapers followed me. My first stop on the campus was the library, which was locked. Remarkably, a janitor walking by had the key. He opened the door, and we choked on the dust that spilled out. It was several inches thick on the ground, and we could see our footprints as we cautiously entered the building. We eventually reached the stacks. Every single book was gone except for those in Russian. Even as recently as the early 1990s, the library had a collection of more than 175,000 books, 3,500 manuscripts and 2,500 rare books, including some original documents from the formation of the country in the 1700s. They had disappeared. It was haunting to see such an absence. The stacks looked like skeletons missing their souls. We all stared in silence for several minutes. It was all gone.

We left the library to go see the kitchens and the dormitories. On the way out, I took $50 worth of Afghanis out of my pocket and asked the janitor to sweep up all of the dust.

Elsewhere on campus, the story repeated itself. Most of the pots and pans in the kitchens were gone, as was all the fuel and any stove or utensil that had not been bolted down. In the dust I found several pans that had holes in them from tank rounds. I could not believe that the fighting had been that severe. There clearly had been no safe quarter in Kabul during the last decade. I later put the pots on exhibition in the library.

When we arrived at the dormitories, we found dead bodies in the dust of the basement in addition to the same physical devastation.

Arriving back in my office, I was starting to have serious doubts that Afghanistan could recover from this trauma. That the country could return from the dark ages. That perhaps it had been dealt a fatal blow from which it could not recover. It was my first week on the job, and the list of absolutely critical projects was spiraling out of control, every one of them imperative to the country. I forced myself to stay calm and tackle each one as best I could with the impossibly limited resources at my disposal. I forced myself not to give into despair. It was not easy.

Reasserting control over Kabul University was critical, it being the historic flagship institution of the country. The president of Kabul University had been appointed by the same mujahideen commander who had invited Osama bin Laden to Afghanistan, whom the Taliban had left alone. My first act was to replace him. Even though I was a government minister, theoretically with the full weight of an internationally backed government behind me, this man was a member of a powerful militia. In actuality, his group may have been stronger than the government in 2001.

Dressed in a suit, I went to his office, where I found him clutching a wood stove and sitting on the ground. There was no desk in his office. There was no lightbulb in his office. There were no books in his office. He did not have any educational degrees, or any background that would allow him to run a university in any direction other than into the ground. I knew no international donor would sit with this man. The president of Kabul University would be the face of education in the new Afghanistan. It could not be this man.

After a brief conversation where I confirmed his lack of experience, I told him brusquely that I was replacing him. I told him I needed someone with experience to run this school. I told him I needed somebody I could trust, who would work with me to modernize and overhaul the entire education system.

His response was indicative of the old Afghanistan. He said he would talk with his mujahideen commanders about this. I told him that wasn't necessary, that I was the minister of higher education, with a wide mandate, and was able to approve and appoint whom I want. He replied that I did not have the authority to replace him. I told him I could remove him today if I wanted to, and was increasingly thinking about it. Understanding my seriousness, he switched gears and asked for two weeks to talk to his commanders. I told him he had one week, and that I would be bringing his replacement by the campus in the next few days. He said he would resist that. I told him it didn't matter what he wanted any more.

True to my word, I brought his replacement by several days later. While the old president watched from his office window, I toured Mr. Akbar Popal, a graduate of the American University of Beirut who had studied agriculture and also obtained a master's degree, around the shelled grounds. The few faculty left on the campus, who had been living in the dormitories with nowhere else to go, excitedly began following us, introducing themselves and gleefully asking when Mr. Popal would begin working. I told them that if Mr. Popal accepted, he could start work as soon as he liked.

It was a monumental task, to completely rehabilitate a university whose physical campus was destroyed, whose library was nonexistent, which had no students, and which was covered in land mines and bullet casings. To my everlasting pleasure, Mr. Popal accepted the challenge on the spot.

The old president, seeing the excitement brought about by simply walking an educated and modern face around the grounds, came to my office the next day. He asked politely if I would refund his fuel expenses from running the wood stove in his office. I said all of his receipts would be reimbursed. He bowed slightly and walked out of the room. I never saw him again.

When I told President Karzai about my plans to reassert government control of education across the rest of the country, he gave me the green light. He also warned me to be careful. I would be treading on the egos of some very powerful and violent people, and he urged me to move with as much diplomacy as possible. I assured him I would.

After replacing the president of Kabul University, I moved on to the next biggest and closest university, Nangarhar University. The university is located in the city of Jalalabad to the east of Kabul on the road to Pakistan. The same story in Kabul repeated itself. A very powerful jihadi figure was in charge who knew very little about education. I confronted him. He was furious. I stayed firm and asserted my control. I eventually replaced him with a highly qualified doctor who had attended medical school in Europe.

Occasionally, I had to go up against truly powerful warlords. In the province of Balkh in the north, I learned that the president of the university was a secretary of a warlord named General Rashid Dostum. Dostum, an ethnic Uzbek, had been trained by the Soviets and fought against the mujahideen in the 1980s before switching sides after the Soviet withdrawal. When the Taliban emerged, he began fighting against them with the old mujahideen commanders he had fought against in the 1980s. While his force accepted government rule in his areas, they never disarmed themselves, and even today he is rumored to have more than 50,000 men under his control.

To effectively replace the president of Balkh University, who was not an academic, I would ultimately need Dostum's support. I did not think he would like the move to replace someone loyal to him in an area his militias controlled.

Increasingly confident in my abilities to effect change in the country, however, I brought my team and a full entourage of bodyguards and advisors to Balkh University. I was determined to impress them with my plans for their university while gently reminding them that I was a minister of the government and fully in charge. Balkh University, being in the north of the country at the very limits of the Taliban's control, had suffered much less destruction of infrastructure than in the south and east. I delivered a lengthy speech to the entire student body and all of the faculty in an auditorium. I talked about renovations of existing buildings, the introduction of new professors and modern teaching methods, and the replacement of professors who were past their prime. I also told the faculty I would be introducing a democratic system by which to elect their new president, whom I would not simply appoint. The faculty was heavily divided between three ethnicities: Pashtun, Hazara and Uzbek. With one group incapable of winning by a simple majority, I knew they would have to work together to pick their president.

The students cheered at my suggestions, and the faculty eagerly embraced my attempts at reform. All that was left was to see what Dostum thought.

Dostum heard about my visit to Balkh University and in a show of his own power, invited my entire delegation, some fifty people, to one of his nearby houses for dinner. After the usual formalities, he and I got to talking about what I was trying to do. He listened intently to my thoughts on education, and to my great surprise, he said he welcomed all of these ideas.

The next day, as we were preparing to return to Kabul, Dostum again invited my delegation over. We arrived at his house to find presents for every single one of us, and he and I again talked at length about education and its importance to the country. I returned to Kabul with his full blessings to do whatever I deemed necessary to improve Balkh University.

I repeated this process until all sixteen public universities in the country were back up and running and firmly under the control of the Ministry of Higher Education. Kandahar University in the south, Balkh University in the north, Nangarhar University in the east, Herat University in the west, Kabul University in the capital, and many others. To have complete ownership of these universities was very important. They, like Afghanistan, were too fragmented, polarized and politicized to be left on their own. They lacked basic resources and each wanted to go its own direction. They had no ability to handle their own administrative affairs, and had few students and fewer teachers. This was not a moment for complete institutional freedom, though I dreamed of a day where each of these universities would be strong enough to stand on its own feet. I thought that after a time of intensive help from our ministry, all of the universities could be subsequently decentralized and left to run their own affairs. But for now, nationwide curriculums needed to be set, teachers hired, and pencils and paper purchased and distributed.

I also worked to start new universities wherever possible. This included Bamiyan University, located near the remains of the giant buddhas. It brought me great joy to help reopen Herat University in the province of my birth. I worked to give them 2,000 acres of land for rapid expansion, and created a master campus plan to provide a framework for that expansion. It is now the third largest university in the country.

My favorite project, however, was to build Kabul Education University, designed solely to produce the teachers Afghanistan so badly needed. I had not forgotten my own time as a professor, when Columbia University had helped establish an education institute in the 1960s. I based this new university around that one. I thought it could be an extension of that program, which had shut down during the fighting in the 1980s.

I established Kabul Education University in a highly symbolic place, on the grounds of what had been, in turn, the headquarters of the Communist party, an office of the Taliban, and a home to Osama bin Laden. Securing such desirable land was difficult, and I again came into contact with mujahideen leaders who threatened me. But the symbolism of turning a former terrorist camp into an education institute was overwhelming. Education had to define the new Afghanistan.

I almost always hailed a taxi to get around Kabul. When I took a taxi to what I hoped would become Kabul Education University, a militia under the control of a powerful mujahideen commander was in charge of it, and refused to let me into the gates. Because I had arrived using a taxi, and was unarmed, the militia did not take me seriously. I eventually returned in a convoy of armored landcruisers and pickup trucks with Afghan commandos who served as my bodyguards. They begrudgingly let me in and, after several frantic phone calls to their commanders, eventually evacuated the compound.

It took me two long years to successfully establish the teachers' school. Today it has more than 5,000 students, the vast majority of whom are female. Each year it graduates trained teachers who are quickly offered jobs at schools around the country.

PRIVATE UNIVERSITIES

It was clear from our planning sessions that even by reopening all of the public universities, Afghanistan would likely not be able to accommodate all of the students in the country, particularly after the next few years. We assumed, correctly, that interest in education would be high. Even as I pushed for the creation of the nation's first private universities, I had no idea just how powerful the attraction of education would prove to be.

The Constitution being drafted after the fall of the Taliban was based on the Constitution that had been used in the 1960s and 1970s. This was a beautiful document, but in terms of education, it was critically lacking in two regards: it made private higher education illegal, and did not allow public universities to charge tuition or housing fees.

Both of those stipulations reflected the state of education in a quiet and peaceful Afghanistan. There was no need for public universities to charge money, because relatively small numbers students attended them. Those fees were easily subsidized by the budgets awarded to the universities from the government. And because there was no overwhelming demand for higher education, there was no need for more institutions, particularly not ones that could not easily be controlled by the government.

I asked the Chief Justice of the Supreme Court, Salam Azimi, who was leading the panel to draft a new Constitution, to give me an audience with the committee. I soon found myself in front of them, and lectured them for two hours on the necessity of allowing private education. I told them that without the safety valve allowed by private education, the public system would quickly be overwhelmed, itself forbidden to charge any fees. They had a lot on their minds as they shaped the new document containing all the rules of the new Afghanistan, an Afghanistan they wanted to respect tradition and allow for growth at the same time. They promised they would seriously consider my proposal.

Several days later, I received a phone call. I had not been able to persuade them to allow public universities to charge tuition, but had successfully convinced them to allow private education. I accepted this as enough of a victory.

My interest in private education initially was to provide more outlets to students as they sought higher education. Later, as I worked to modernize and improve universities already under my ministry's control, I realized they could have a second function: to be bastions of reform in a country extremely resistant to change. If private universities began to become more desirable to students than public universities, public schools would be forced to change to keep up.

Despite the enthusiasm with which most of my reforms were accepted, there was pushback, sometimes from where I least expected it.

WOMEN'S EDUCATION

Kabul University had always been coeducational, from the day it opened its doors in the early 1930s until the Taliban banned women from receiving an education. And yet when I went to reopen the university, a long line of people advised me to not allow men and women to sit in the same classroom. They were advisors to President Karzai, they were fellow ministers, they were even Afghan-Americans. Some of them even said there should be a shift system, whereby women would go to class during the day and the men would go to class at night. I was amazed to find myself one of the very few advocates of coeducation, which, much as its opponents tried to claim, was not hopelessly progressive. It was restorative. It was the resumption of normalcy in a country devoid of it. It was the return of fairness and equality, the return of values that my generation had been born with and accepted.

Shocked by the resistance to equal female education from most corners, I became quite militant on the issue. This was well before the Western world determined that higher education could be an area of massive growth and began supporting it. I had traveled repeatedly to Western donor agencies across the US, Europe, and Asia to plead for more resources to invest in higher education, and had been roundly rejected. They all said they would start only with elementary schools. This made sense at the moment, as building an elementary school requires few resources and can be accomplished quickly. I begged them to look down the road, to plan for the future. The best answer I got said that they would consider funding higher education in several years. I found myself ignored by the international community and threatened by conservative elements of Afghan society.

Determined to have women receive an equal education alongside their male counterparts and exasperated by my lack of support on a subject I considered a nonstarter, I pushed through a highly controversial executive order several months before the first intake of new students into public universities: every single female who applied to a public university would be accepted.

I had put immense thought into this, and wrestled for months with the complexities, both philosophical and mundane. First, how many college-age females do we have in the country? Nobody knew, because no census had been taken in decades. What if x percent of them apply; do we have enough seats for them? Enough paper? What about 2x? Thinking more generally, do we do this once or do we do it again next year? Is this fundamentally fair or is it bending the rules? How will different segments of society react? Will women even go for this?

It was a staggering success. Tens of thousands of women applied and every single one of them was accepted, for the first time grabbing hold of something that had been denied to them either by an imported Taliban mindset or by ignorance. There was, despite threats to the contrary, no violence anywhere in the country on the first day of classes. The Taliban had fled, and I was determined to continue the assault on their imported and backward ideas that had no place in my country. I had become, and have remained, a staunch militant in the cause of a quality education for all.

There were of course problems with adjusting the system to handle a very subpar intake of uneducated people, but in the first few years, these problems were shared equally by men and women. Many students could not read or write their own language. From areas where the Taliban had held the strongest control, there were no female students, because no females who had gone to school in recent memory. Most could not point to their country on a map, or had never heard of some of the provinces. The vast majority of them were refugees, either in their own country or returning from Pakistan and Iran. There was an enormous burden placed on the professors in those years, but by and large they responded with patience and kindness.

Today, the issue of coeducational universities is once again accepted among the vast majority of the population. People eventually realized that far from trying to import foreign ideas into the classroom, I was working merely to restore what had once existed there.

Bigger than these challenges, however, was my limited budget. I was given six million dollars for the 2002-2003 year, and then tasked with rebuilding higher education. Given that most campuses had been completely destroyed and that the first step was to physically rebuild and repair buildings, this was a hopelessly low amount of money. Because none of the public universities could charge tuition, even $100 as an annual administrative fee, this sum represented the entire amount of money I had to pay for teacher salaries, building maintenance, student textbooks, new books for libraries, grounds crews, computers, administrative staff, separate male and female dormitories and security.

While almost all international donors ignored my calls for more funding, both for the Afghan government and for individual universities, Germany did not. They took the long view and understood the importance of well-staffed universities that were, at the least, clean, safe, and full of the necessary supplies. They helped me and the ministry considerably with our work. They augmented our meager budget by funding programs that delivered tangible results, like IT training, while understanding that education is not an area that can be easily quantified beyond the number of male and female students. Its results take time to show.

Or at least they usually do. While education would go on to be a buzzword for Western development specialists later in the decade, the Afghan population, from every province, beat them to the punch.

Regardless of who is running the country, village elders from some of the most remote places on earth are always coming to Kabul to meet government ministers and the president and present them with a list of demands. In true Afghan fashion, more than half are wildly unreasonable. Their requests run the gamut of asking for an airport to be dedicated to their village of 50 people with direct flights from Kabul to asking for three more cows to produce milk.

Starting in 2003, these elders had all added something else to their lists: a university. From Paktika, from Uruzgan, from Ghor, from some of the most conservative or neglected places in Afghanistan, these elders came to ask for universities. I was quite surprised to hear this from President Karzai, who told me about it during a conference call. He asked me to attend some of the meetings, and to my everlasting astonishment, I watched illiterate, uneducated and fiercely conservative men plead with President Karzai for a university in their provinces. The same men who had resisted education even before the Taliban made the idea popular were now asking how long it would take to build one and open the doors. President Karzai would direct them to talk to me, and my first task was always to lower their expectations. I told them that while I could not open a medical university by the start of the coming week, I could start an agricultural school to teach basic farming techniques within three months. They were always disappointed in not getting their medical university, but always accepted my schools when I offered them. And to my continued amazement, I found myself building networks of schools around the country, in some of the most remote places imaginable, with the full support of people I had thought would find what I was doing completely unacceptable.

This kind of demand had never existed in Afghanistan before, not even when I was born here. This validated my assumption that education could be a major component of what the new Afghanistan could be proud of. That education could be something that defined the new generation. It validated my theory that after having been deprived of it for so long, the people of Afghanistan would wholly embrace education. If there was any silver lining to the Taliban regime, it was that by condemning the Afghan people to ignorance, they paved the way for a whole generation of people who would carry the torch of learning far and wide.

PAKISTAN

The allure of education was even powerful enough to pull in Afghanistan's most problematic neighbor: Pakistan. I was surprised when on one morning my secretary told me representatives from the Pakistani government were waiting outside my office. I let them wait for a few minutes and composed my thoughts. I had no idea what they could want with me.

They had been sent to me as part of a goodwill mission, and they quickly got to the point: they had three million dollars bookmarked to support Afghan higher education. I immediately proposed a building on the campus of Kabul University to be named after a great Pakistani poet known to all Afghans and Iranians but, surprisingly, not to the delegation.

Mohammad Iqbal Lahoori was a philosopher, poet, and politician who lived in Lahore, India, which became part of the newly created country of Pakistan in 1947. For his work he would be knighted by King George v before his death in 1938. While a native Urdu speaker, he wrote most of his poetry in Dari, one of the two languages of Afghanistan, the language he considered to be the sweetest he knew of. His poetry was appreciated in as different circles as us Supreme Court justices and Soviet bureaucrats, and he was widely known as the Poet of the East. While he worked hard in his later years to urge on the creation of an all Muslim state, he died before Pakistan became a reality.

He was an ideal figure to become a symbol of Afghan-Pakistani friendship because, in 1932, he had attended the formal dedication of Kabul University as an invitee of King Zahir Shah.

I told them they could have this building, named after a Pakistani patriot and poet, built at Kabul University with one condition: They had to double their funding. I could build a good building for three million dollars, but I could build a great structure that would stand the test of time for six million. The team smiled and said they had to report back to Islamabad and would let me know in a few days.

A few days later they came back and said it was a deal. Today the Mohammad Iqbal Lahoori Arts and Sciences building is the biggest building at Kabul University, with his name featured prominently across the front.

I hope that someday in the future that Afghanistan and Pakistan can have a productive relationship. We have so much shared history.

Epilogue

THE AMERICAN UNIVERSITY OF AFGHANISTAN

After my work as minister finished, I stayed on in Kabul to begin work on my biggest dream: an American University of Afghanistan. While other ex-ministers choose the colors for their new mansions in Dubai, having stolen obscene amounts of money from international donors and the Afghan people, I installed myself in a bullet riddled house with no electricity on the outskirts of Kabul and began the slow and fitful process of creating an entirely new kind of university. A kind of university Afghanistan had never seen before.

An entire generation of Afghan intellectuals and civil servants born in the 1950s and 1960s had traveled abroad to receive their education. Some of them had gone to one of the three American universities in the Middle East at the time: the American University of Beirut, the Lebanese-American University, and the American University of Cairo. Others had gone on to Europe, while others traveled all the way to the United States.

With Afghanistan now excited by the prospect of quality higher education and with the international community working to develop the country, the time seemed right for a university that would employ the best international professors we could find. This would be a gift to the Afghan people, promising the best education possible and acting as a symbol of what I, and so many other Afghans, had come to love about America: its higher education system.

Like Kabul University with its international partnerships in the 1960s, this would bring international faculty from around the world to lecture in English to the smartest students in the country. They would teach according to the standards used at top universities in Europe and the US. Unlike temporary partnerships with international universities, this would be a permanent institution. It would be founded and run largely by Afghans in close coordination with foreign professors and staff.

Working with an accomplished group of Afghans and Americans, we spent two years fighting for funding, space, and land, going up against everyone from conservative members of parliament to Western education specialists who told me, in hushed tones, that Afghanistan was not ready for such a place, all the while praising education as they key to the country's future. I didn't mind being ignored or attacked by old mujahideen commanders with no interest in sending their daughters school, but I could not help but take it personally every time a foreigner told me that Afghans weren't smart enough for what we were doing. That we were moving too fast.

Those same Western specialists also told us repeatedly to change the name. The most polite of them said it was simply a relic of a bygone era from when America was a more neutral entity in this part of the world, while the most aggressive told me it was too political. They are both wrong. Despite everything that has happened in Afghanistan, Central Asia, the Middle East, and across the Muslim world, America, almost remarkably, is seen as the best place in the world to get a university education. It was always amusing to point this out to leading Americans who, often from their lofty think-tank posts in Washington, DC, told me what we were doing simply would not work, and that our ideas were wrong.

The results speak for themselves. In 2014, more than one thousand seven hundred full and part time students attend classes at the American University of Afghanistan, which started with less than forty. In a country where female illiteracy tops eighty percent and severe cultural barriers prohibit many fathers from sending their daughters to school, let alone a school whose name shares a distant connection to the American government and has soldiers in my country, more than thirty percent of the students are female. Its student finances operate on what we call the Robin Hood system, where rich students pay an expensive tuition, which is used largely to subsidize education for the seventy percent of our students who cannot afford to pay. We have fulfilled one of the mandates we set down before we admitted our first student, to be a truly national university; we have students from all thirty-four provinces in Afghanistan, including the most dangerous and most remote. We have land in the four other major urban centers in Afghanistan, and opened our first branch campus in my home province of Herat. Our next branch campus opened in Kandahar, the so-called spiritual home of the Taliban. We have celebrated four graduations and produced 29 Fulbright scholars. More than sixty internationals work at the university, and of the forty international professors in our academic programs, thirty seven percent of them have PhDs. Students have, completely on their own, founded a wide variety of student clubs, from astronomy to photography to Model United Nations. We have partnerships with Stanford University's School of Law, which has law fellows permanently on campus and has helped us roll out an undergraduate law degree based on the British system, as well as Georgetown University and the University of California at San Diego. We introduced the nation's first Master of Business Administration to great fanfare in 2011, which resulted in Afghan businesses sending their management to us for training. We also train Afghan employees from the Ministry of Foreign Affairs, the Ministry of Justice, the Attorney General's Office, the Ministry of the Interior, the Ministry of Education, and the Ministry of Mines, among others. We also work with the embassies of more than a dozen countries to educate their Afghan staff. While we operate on a modest five acre campus built and operated by the American International High School in the 1960s and 1970s, we have eighty square acres across the street that house our ever expanding program offerings, including a women's center for economic development and a business innovation center.

This university is making the difference that will decide the future of this country. While I cannot say whether the next leader of the country will come from this specific school, I can say that he or she is likely to emerge from one of the universities the West has supported here.

From the bottom of my heart, I thank those Afghan businessmen, who know who they are, as well as the American and Western governments who have so graciously helped us get off the ground. We have a lot of work left, but we are making real, tangible progress.

THE TALIBAN AND THE FUTURE

People often ask me my thoughts on the future of the country, which is another way of asking what they think the Taliban will do. My reply, repeated ad nauseam for close to a decade, is that while a core of the Taliban will likely never stop fighting, many of them will upon the departure of foreign soldiers from the country. For the remainder, they can only become less and less relevant and Afghans themselves must lead the fight against them. While history is an uncertain guide in Afghanistan, it does show us that those who are hailed by the population as freedom fighters one day can quickly be seen as warlords the next day. Those same popular mujahideen who victoriously expelled the Soviets are the same people who then cut the country to pieces and are now reviled by Afghans today. With the departure of most of the foreign soldiers in the next few years, that pivotal switch in attitudes is likely to occur again. If the West maintains a quiet hand in Afghan affairs from afar and capitalizes on this, the country can be saved.

TO THE DIASPORA

My fellow Afghans, wherever you are, I urge you to return home to your watan. This country needs your help, and the difference you can make here is astonishing. If you are unsure where to start, I will help you.

www.ingramcontent.com/pod-product-compliance
Ingram Content Group UK Ltd.
Pitfield, Milton Keynes, MK11 3LW, UK
UKHW021933190726
13853UKWH00004B/1412

9 783944 214184